ON THE MOVE

ON THE MOVE

A History of the Hispanic Church in the United States

Moises Sandoval

ORBIS BOOKS

Maryknoll, New York 10545

Copyright © 1990 by Moises Sandoval
Published by Orbis Books, Maryknoll, NY 10545
Manufactured in the United States of America
All rights reserved

Library of Congress Cataloging-in-Publication Data

Sandoval, Moises.
 On the move: a history of the Hispanic church in the United
States / Moises Sandoval.
 p. cm.
 Includes bibliographical references.
 ISBN 0-88344-675-8
 1. Hispanic Americans—Religion. 2. Hispanic American Catholics—
History. 3. United States—Church history. I. Title.
BR563.H57S26 1990
277.3′008968—dc20

 90-33440
 CIP

Contents

Part III: The Church of the Poor Comes of Age

Foreword

Moises Sandoval has already proven himself as an able historian of the church and the Hispanic peoples of the United States. In 1983 he edited and wrote a major portion of *Fronteras: A History of the Hispanic American Church in the U.S.A. since 1513* (published by the Mexican American Cultural Center). *Fronteras* was the first attempt to reflect on a topic that has hardly received the attention of historians in the United States. The history of the Catholic Church in the United States is usually written from the perspective of groups other than Hispanic and other minorities. Such histories usually begin with the church in the eighteenth century in the northeast of the United States. The works of Mr. Sandoval are therefore a welcome addition to the unfolding story of the church in this country.

The reader will be impressed by data that has up to now remained unpublished. But perhaps what will have the most impact in this book will be the critical style with which Mr. Sandoval approaches the subject. The historiographical approach of this study has come from the liberationist perspective and is very much in keeping with historical literature currently being published by CEHILA (the Commission for the Study of the History of the Church in Latin America), an organization of historians and social scientists from throughout Latin America; it has been in existence for over fifteen years and continues to produce books and papers every year. The intent of CEHILA is to look at church history from the perspective of the poor and oppressed peoples. One of the premises is that history is usually written by the victors and not by the losers. All too often history is recorded by those who had the upper hand, while the equally heroic story of those who lost out is overlooked.

This book holds the church in the U.S. accountable to its

approaches to the Hispanic presence in many areas, particularly in the area of social concern. While the language is critical, it is not condemnatory; the author clearly writes from a knowledgeable appreciation of past events and holds church leadership accountable to its prophetic mission. This is especially true in his treatment of twentieth-century events.

Any treatment, be it historical, political, social, or cultural, of Hispanic peoples runs into the challenge presented by the wide variety within the total Hispanic spectrum. Geography is greatly responsible for this. The Spanish missions in northern New Mexico, because of their location, far from the mainstream and from the political centers of power of church life, necessarily developed a unique flavor and style of church spirituality. The Caribbean church (the roots of many of the non-Mexican American Catholics) well into the twentieth century, maintained strong, close ties to Spain. Puerto Rican Catholics, whether in New York or on the Island, have had an experience of church quite different from that of other Hispanic Americans. The Cuban American experience also deserves special treatment— especially the events leading to and beyond the immigration experience of the 1960s. In providing the story of the church and the Cuban Americans, this book fills a gap in the *Fronteras* volume.

The struggle of Hispanic Americans to maintain their cultural-religious character has gone hand in hand with the social-economic-political struggle. This book presents a saga still in the making of a people who, like other identifiable ethnic groups, has had to overcome the challenges of discrimination and racial prejudice. Unfortunately the institutional church has not always been there to champion the causes of justice and civil rights among minorities, including those of Hispanics. Individuals in leadership positions and some religious communities in the first half of the twentieth century did take heroic stands, but it was not until the 1940s that the church, as a national and regional institution, began to recognize its role and participate in the struggle.

There are parts of this book that are not pleasant to read, but what is offered here is crucial if we are to avoid the pitfalls of the past. Knowing Mr. Sandoval and his contributions to the life of the church over many years as a Catholic journalist and editor of *Maryknoll* and *Revista Maryknoll*, I know of his deep love and respect for the church, including its hierarchy. He writes a strong line, but out of an equally strong regard for the church's present and future, over which this generation of Catholics has responsibility.

It is my prayer and hope that this book will find wide readership, that it will spark continued documentation, research, and writing on a topic that is as fascinating as it is challenging.

Ricardo Ramirez, CSB
Bishop of Las Cruces, New Mexico

Acknowledgments

I am grateful, first of all, to Dr. Enrique Dussel, president of the Commission for Historical Studies of the Church in Latin America (CEHILA), who urged us Hispanics in the United States to write our own history in the church and, more importantly, convinced us that we could do it.

Next, I am indebted to Bishop Ricardo Ramirez, who has always encouraged me in my writing and offered helpful suggestions on this book. Father Bob Wright, O.M.I., of Oblate School of Theology in San Antonio, Texas, contributed an invaluable critique on the section dealing with the nineteenth century and generously shared his own research and library.

Father Juan Romero, a fellow New Mexican and long-time collaborator, went through the manuscript page by page with the thoroughness and dedication one can expect only from an old friend.

I owe special thanks to Peggy Ellsberg, who helped me smooth out the rough edges, and to Robert Ellsberg for editing the manuscript. There were, however, many other priests, bishops, Sisters, and lay persons in Hispanic ministry who shared insights and information.

My biggest debt, however, is to Penny, my wife, friend, and companion, who has always supported me and provided the home environment that allowed me to devote the many evenings and weekends and the travel that have been part of the process of producing this modest work.

Introduction

The option for the poor, embraced so emphatically by the Latin American bishops at their meeting at Medellín, Colombia, in 1968, at Puebla, Mexico, in 1979, and, in a less dramatic way, by many U.S. bishops has challenged historians to write a new kind of church history emphasizing the religious experience of the poor.

Traditional church history has been written from the perspective of the institutional church, the cardinals, bishops, secular and religious clergy, and to a lesser extent, the women's congregations. It has been written from the perspective of people who wield power. To the extent that such accounts focus on the laity, they deal with the experience, views, and interests of the economic and political elite. The experience of the poor, and especially that of minorities, is ignored. This is as true in the United States as it is in Latin America.

Church historians in the United States have given little attention to Hispanics. Though the Catholic Church had been firmly rooted in the Southwest for 250 years when the United States seized that region from Mexico in 1846, most historians imply that the church was really established by the non-Hispanic bishops and clergy who came after the conquest. Whenever Hispanics are mentioned in those histories, their religious expression is often demeaned; whenever there is controversy, their point of view is left out. Parish histories, even in places where Hispanics are now the majority, seldom mention them. It is as if they did not exist.

As a consequence, there is great ignorance about Hispanics in the church, extending not only to their past and current religious contributions but even to their very existence. Not long ago, a bishop from a North Central state wrote to the Secretariat for Hispanic Affairs of the National Conference of Catholic Bishops: "Most of our people are unaware of the Hispanic presence, and if they are aware, they carry prejudice and misinformation about them."

With this volume, I hope to contribute to building a new awareness of the past and present role of Hispanics and of their promise for the future, especially in view of the fact that they will be the majority of Catholics in the United States in ten or fifteen years. Historically, the church has not served its Hispanic members well. But in every period there have been a few—a bishop here, a few clergy and religious there, and unacknowledged lay ministers—who have served these abandoned people. In recent years, a church of the poor has appeared, making that special option that the gospel demands. It is the slow rise of this church that this book attempts to chronicle.

This book is a small part of the ambitious vision of the Commission for the Study of the History of the Church in Latin America (CEHILA). For fifteen years these historians, theologians, sociologists, and experts in other disciplines have been writing a new history of the church from the perspective of the poor. The first project was a general history in ten volumes, one of which dealt with the Hispanic Church north of the Rio Grande (Moises Sandoval, ed., *Fronteras: A History of the Latin American Church in the U.S.A. since 1513* [San Antonio: Mexican American Cultural Center, 1983]). This current book is part of a series of mini-histories which will appear in the next few years. The U.S. Hispanic church is considered part of this "Latin American" project partly because of its Iberian roots but also because many of its members are immigrants from Latin America.

This volume is divided into three parts: (1) discovery, settlement, and evangelization (1513–1846); (2) the American conquest and the implanting of a melting-pot church (1846–1946); and (3) the coming of age of a church of the poor (1946 to the present). The poor in the beginning included the indigenous peoples subjected to an evangelization that demanded the surrender of their own religious beliefs and way of life, and the acceptance of the religion and culture of their conquerors.

Though this book spans a long period, I feel that, in a sense, I have experienced much of it. I was born in 1930 in a part of

New Mexico that has been described as being a hundred years behind the times. The place, called Terromote, consisted of small ranches located in the foothills of the eastern side of the Sangre de Cristo mountains north of Santa Fe. Horse-drawn wagons were the usual mode of transportation and the roads were dirt lanes which became almost impassable in bad weather. The inhabitants were all Hispanics who spoke almost exclusively an archaic form of Spanish. The pastor from the nearest parish came to celebrate Mass in the community chapel only a few times a year. He seldom tarried afterward. We were evangelized by our families and by the *Penitentes*, a lay society of uncertain origins who practiced rigorous penance.

The *Penitentes* led the daily life of the church in those isolated communities. They conducted burials and other prayer services, including the ceremonies of Holy Week, complete with a rather realistic reenactment of the crucifixion. The Good Friday service was interminable but we, as children, looked forward to the procession from the chapel to meet the *Penitentes* coming from the *morada*, or meeting house. What fascinated us was that one of the *Penitentes,* dressed only in a loincloth, carried a heavy cross. The two groups stopped about fifty yards apart and there followed a long series of *alabados* (hymns), with one side singing a response. We youngsters tried to get a glimpse of the "naked man" carrying the cross, as he was shielded by his fellow *Penitentes.*

From there our family moved to Colorado, where we experienced the religious life of a despised minority, welcome in the parish church only at certain times, and often the objects of hostility from the Anglo members. We learned then what it meant to be part of a church that did not want us.

Later, I personally witnessed some of the beginnings of the church of the poor. I accompanied a bishop and several clergy from religious orders who went to stand on the picket lines with farmworkers in California. I attended some of the joyful fiestas marking the episcopal ordination of some of the Hispanic bishops. I was at all three national Encuentros, where Hispanics gathered to express their demands of the mother church and to begin to outline a plan for Hispanic ministry. I attended some of the meetings of PADRES (Priests Associated for Religious,

Educational, and Social Rights), who were so instrumental in the struggle of Hispanics for a place in the church. In many cases, therefore, this is a book about events I witnessed.

The religious experience of the Hispanic church, poor in part because it has lacked resources but more so because it has been powerless and despised, challenges the larger church not just to serve but to accept it as a full partner. That means creating a new model of church, one that is open to the contributions of cultures and classes of people previously ignored or even despised.

PART I

Discovery
to Evangelization
(1513–1846)

—1—

The People of the Land

The Indians the Spaniards encountered in territories now part of the United States were on the periphery of North American civilization. They were primitive not only in comparison to Europeans but in comparison to some of their contemporaries in the Americas. In the southern part of the continent the Spaniards found two advanced cultures, the Maya and the Aztec. At their zenith, these people were as accomplished as other advanced societies anywhere in the world. The Maya, for example, had mathematical concepts more advanced than those of the Greeks. Their calendars were among the most accurate in the world. Their skill at building with stone still amazes people who visit their temples in Yucatan and Guatemala. Their temples and pyramids are marvels of stone masonry and architecture.

Unlike the Maya, who had fallen victim to some catastrophe and were in decline, the Aztec were at their zenith when the Spaniards came. They ruled over a wide area now part of Mexico and Guatemala. Heirs to other advanced civilizations, the Teotihuacan, Toltec, Mixtec, and Zapotec, the Aztec were skilled in agriculture, stone masonry, and metalwork. They had a complex religion and social system.

Between one and two million Indians lived in the rest of North America. They were beyond the influence and control of the Aztec empire. In the frigid areas of the North, nomads moved from place to place in search of food, surviving by hunting and fishing. Some of these nomadic tribes lived in territories now in the United States. The Penuti inhabited the Sacramento and San Joaquin valleys; the Lutuma, northwestern California. The rest of them, from California to Florida, were planters before the Spaniards came. Nevertheless, in time many inhabitants of the plains and Southwest reverted to a nomadic life. This was made possible by the horse, which the Spaniards introduced into the New World. When horses became available to the Indians, they no longer needed to plant. The horse made it easy for them to follow and hunt the buffalo herds. They traded some of the meat for corn and squash grown by sedentary tribes like the Pueblos.

Excluding the Eskimos, there were six major cultural groups: those on the Northwest coast, on the plains, on the plateaus, eastern woodlands, the northern area, and the Southwest. The main language groups were the Aztec-Tanoan, Algonquian-Wakashan, and Hokan-Siouan. (The Aztec-Tanoan were related to the tribe that ruled central Mexico.) There were many variations within those language groups.

There were hundreds of tribes. East of the Mississippi, the Spaniards met the Caddos, Muscogi, and Timicua; in the high plains, the Wichitas and the Comanches; in the Southwest, pueblo tribes like the Zuni and the Tewa, and other Indians like the Apache and the Papago.

In the Southwest, the earliest known inhabitants were the Cochise (c. 8,000 B.C.E.). They, in turn, gave way to the Mogollon. Between 5,000 and 1,000 B.C.E., manioc, maize, beans, and squash were domesticated in North and South America. The Pueblos, who reached their zenith between 1300 and 900 B.C.E., were prosperous and well-organized, the men and women modestly dressed. They were skilled weavers and potters, makers of turquoise and coral jewelry. One of their ethnic branches, the Zuni, built the fabled seven cities of Cibola, of which only Acoma remains. Life for all the Indians living on territories now part of the United States was elemental, however, a struggle for land, for food, for security. Warfare with other tribes was constant.

The advanced societies at the time the Spaniards arrived were the ones most susceptible to conquest. They had accumulated riches such as gold, silver, and precious stones that were of great value to their conquerors. Also, they had skills that the Spaniards could utilize. They had expertise in architecture, construction, hydraulics, agriculture, working with stone, ceramics, and even metal. Their buildings and other properties were useful to their conquerors. Since the Aztec ruled a large area, the Spaniards had only to defeat the rulers to gain control over vast territories. Furthermore, the Aztec in particular had a religious belief about the return of a god that facilitated the conquest. They thought at first that the Spaniards were gods.

The myriad groups living in what is now the United States presented a different story. They possessed no riches that the Spaniards coveted. Since they planted only for subsistence, they had no large stores of food. Also, they had negligible skills. For hundreds of years, in some cases, poverty saved them from being conquered.

More significant, they were divided into so many groups that control was not easy to establish, especially among nomadic tribes. The most susceptible to conquest were the Pueblo Indians, because they were the most settled and were not as warlike as other tribes. The Spaniards could put them to work growing crops and raising livestock or fighting hostile tribes. In New Mexico, many Pueblo Indians fought for the Spaniards. Even with Indian help, the *conquistadores* were unable to subjugate all the indigenous peoples of the United States. After 200 years of struggle, they still controlled only pockets of territory, even in the Southwest. The area was too vast, the tribes too numerous, the terrain too inhospitable or remote and the conquerors too few. Peace, when it existed with any group, was always tenuous. Missions might operate for a time, only to be overrun by a new uprising. This was true everywhere, but particularly in Texas and Arizona.

The political organization of a particular tribe was simple. It was led by one or more chiefs. There were associations of various kinds for warriors, the leaders of religious rituals and ceremonies, the medicine men, the heads of various totemic cults, animal or mineral. The style of life was communal. In most tribes, the basic unit of society was a monogamous family, though there were a few tribes that practiced polygamy. For the most part, their broad sense of social morality—on such questions as murder or adultery, for example—was similar to that of their conquerors. Their worldview consisted of a cosmic dualism. Spring struggled against winter, the sun against the moon. There were spirits and demons, and numerous mythologies.

Prairie Indians, who lived west of the Mississippi, divided their camps and villages into two parts, representing earth and sky. The sky was the masculine principle, the earth the feminine. There was a supreme being, the organizer of the land. For some the earth was the supreme being.

The Pueblos worshipped some spirits and feared others. Their ceremonial life had frequent rituals. They believed supernatural forces controlled their lives and had to be propitiated to insure success in hunting and farming and to ward off illness or enemies. The *kachina* cult represented supernatural beings who may have been ancestral spirits. The people worshipped a supreme being, the sun god of the nomads but equally the mother earth of the planters. The jaguar, god of the hunters, had a special place in their pantheon.

The Pueblos had guilds or associations for healers, hunters, warriors, religious, and social leaders. The religious associations carried out the ceremonial life, usually in *kivas*—theaters or dormitories for unmarried males. The Indians believed life after death would be similar to life on earth. They could not accept that as a consequence of how they lived on earth, they could be tortured in hell for all eternity.

Though some groups would be Christianized, rarely would they give up all their native beliefs. Others, on the other hand, would reject the new religion altogether. Still others would accept it for a time, only to return to old beliefs. Christianity was established but its hold would be tenuous.

—2—

Settlement and Evangelization

The landing of Columbus in the New World in 1492 opened the greatest era of exploration, conquest, and evangelization in the history of the world. Within the span of fifty to seventy-five years, most of the Western Hemisphere would come under the control of European nations. For the indigenous peoples they found here, however, it would be the beginning of a long decline that would decimate many tribes.

On April 2, 1513, the explorer Juan Ponce de Leon came ashore on the east coast of Florida near the present site of St. Augustine. Because it was the Easter season, he named the new land *La Gran Pascua Florida*, the Spanish name for that feast.

Ponce de Leon, who had conquered Puerto Rico, was looking for the island of Bimini, where Indian legend had it that there was a fountain of youth. It's doubtful this veteran military man placed much stock in magic fountains. He had fought against the Moors in Spain, helped conquer Hispaniola and then Puerto Rico, where he had found gold and become wealthy. Rather than chasing legends, he looked for new worlds to conquer.

Finding the Indians hostile, the Spaniards reboarded their ships and sailed south along the coast of Florida—which they took to be an island—and then north, where they also landed briefly. Returning to Puerto Rico, Ponce de Leon soon afterward sailed for Spain where he received a patent to colonize Florida. It directed him to submit the Indians to the Catholic faith and to the authority of the Spanish crown. When he returned to Puerto Rico Indian conflicts delayed him. Not until 1521 was he able to mount a second expedition. With 200 men and 50 horses he landed on the west coast of Florida, probably near present-day Tampa. But the settlers were immediately attacked by Indians and Ponce de Leon was wounded by an arrow. Abandoning the project, the expedition went to Cuba where Ponce de Leon died.

At that time Hernán Cortez was conquering Mexico and seizing its riches. The wealth of the Incas would not be discovered for another decade. But some of those treasures would soon be passing through the Florida straits en route to Spain. The prime motive for establishing settlements in Florida was to protect the sea lanes. Though the discovery of great riches in Mexico and Peru caused some of the explorers of Florida to look for wealthy kingdoms, they saw no evidence of precious metals. Moreover, they considered the soil infertile and the prospect of settlement, due to the hostility of the Indians, a daunting task. But it was not zeal to preach the gospel that brought them there.

This is not to say that religion was unimportant. Just as the United States has felt compelled to implant its economic and political system in other parts of the world, the Spaniards felt they had a mandate to spread Catholicism. Spain, after all, was the leading Catholic nation in the world. It had stopped Islam after an 800-year struggle. It had championed the Inquisition and the Counter-Reformation. The names the Spaniards gave to the places they discovered demonstrated how prominent religion was in their worldview. They named them for saints and the central mysteries of their religion: St. Augustine, San Antonio, San Diego, Santa Fe, and Santa Cruz, to name a few. When they saw the rugged mountains of the West, their reddish tinge reminded them of the blood of Christ, and hence the name *Sangre de Cristo*.

For the Spaniards, the state had the duty to evangelize. The crown appointed bishops and religious superiors, decided what priests would come to the New World, paid the salaries of the clergy, and created new dioceses. Moreover, evangelization was part of the process of conquest. The Spaniards saw religion as an interminable conflict between the kingdom of God and the dominion of the devil. They had no compunction about using force to impose Catholicism.

OTHER EXPEDITIONS TO FLORIDA

In 1526, another expedition with 600 colonists, headed by Captain Lucas Vasquez de Ayllon, set out for Florida. Ayllon and Francisco Gordillo had stopped there previously, seizing 150 Indians to make them slaves. Perhaps that in part explains the hostility of the Indians. This time, however, Ayllon went far beyond Florida. He established a colony alongside Chesapeake Bay. But a pestilential fever and a revolt by Indian and black slaves killed many of the colonists, including Ayllon. The 150 who survived returned to Hispaniola in 1527.

The same year, Panfilo de Narvaez set out for Florida with 600 colonists and several Franciscan missioners. After landing on the gulf coast, he divided his force. One half marched inland under the command of Narvaez searching for a wealthy kingdom, which he did not find. The other half continued up the coast by ship. Upon returning to the coast, Narvaez and his men could not find the ships and therefore constructed makeshift boats to return home. Driven off course, they shipwrecked on Galveston Island, where Indians enslaved the survivors. That ill-fated expedition would lead to the exploration and settlement of the Southwest.

More than ten years later, in 1538, Hernando de Soto led another expedition to Tampa Bay. From there he explored the Carolinas, Georgia, Alabama, and Louisiana. Wounded in a battle with Indians, he died on May 21, 1542, as the expedition reached the Mississippi River. He was buried on its banks. His men went on to visit lands now known as Arkansas, Texas, and Oklahoma.

In 1549, Dominican Friar Luis Cancer de Barbastro received permission to lead the spiritual conquest of Florida. With typical bravery—or foolhardiness—Father Diego Tolsa went ashore without armed escort. When a companion brought back word that he had been killed by the Indians, Father Cancer demanded to be put ashore. The captain refused, but Cancer jumped into the water and swam ashore. On a small rise, in full view of the crew of the ship, the Indians surrounded Cancer and killed him with knives and tomahawks as he knelt in prayer. The Dominicans made another attempt in 1555, but a hurricane sank half the ships as they headed for Pensacola. After that, the Crown discouraged other efforts to resettle until the French started a colony on the St. Johns River in 1564.

In 1565, Pedro Menendez de Aviles established St. Augustine after destroying the French fort. This was the first permanent European settlement — and mission — on land now in the United States. Pensacola, the second Spanish colony in Florida, was established in 1696. The Spaniards founded about a dozen settlements in Florida.

NEW MEXICO, TEXAS, ARIZONA, AND CALIFORNIA

The exploration of the Southwest began when four members of the Narvaez expedition, who had shipwrecked on Galveston Island, escaped to the mainland after being enslaved for about seven years. They were Alvar Nuñez Cabeza de Vaca, Alonso del Castillo Maldonado, Andres Dorantes and an Arab or black identified only as Estevánico. After gaining their freedom they walked across what is now Texas, New Mexico, and Arizona. In 1536, they turned up in Culiacan, Mexico, reporting that the Indians had told them of a kingdom called Cibola that had seven cities with great riches.

The news that Nuñez Cabeza de Vaca brought to Mexico about vast riches in Cibola soon mobilized the Spaniards. Three years later, in 1539, Fray Marcos de Niza, accompanied by Estevánico, visited New Mexico and returned with the news that he had actually seen one of the fabled seven cities of Cibola.

The following year, in 1540, Francisco Vasquez de Coronado led an expedition of 300 Spaniards and 800 Indian allies northward. In two years they explored territories now known as Arizona, New Mexico, Oklahoma, and Kansas. They found only poor Indian villages and not the rich kingdom envisioned with eager anticipation as a "new Mexico." Disappointed, Coronado returned to Mexico in 1542, but four missionaries, three priests, and a religious Brother, remained in different villages to evangelize the Indians. The priests were killed but the Brother returned to Mexico with the news of their death. For half a century thereafter the Spaniards showed no further interest in

New Mexico. Poverty had given the Indians a reprieve.

In the 1580s, however, small groups began to venture north. In 1581 Franciscan Brother Agustin Rodriguez and Fathers Francisco López and Juan de Santa María, accompanied by nine soldiers, came up the Rio Grande looking for "a great harvest of souls." For a year they visited as far north as Taos, east to Pecos and west to Acoma and Zuni. Returning home alone with the news of their discoveries, Santa María was killed by the Indians. In 1582, Antonio de Espejo led a small expedition to find out what had happened to the other missioners. He returned with the report that they had been killed. Espejo, however, reported that there were good mining sites in New Mexico.

In 1598, Juan de Oñate began the colonization of New Mexico with 400 settlers, among whom were 138 women and children. On the feast of the Ascension, in the vicinity of present-day El Paso, he took possession of the territory for God and King Philip of Spain. Eight Franciscans and three Mexican Indians who had not taken their final vows were also part of the expedition.

California was discovered the same year that Coronado was returning from the plains empty-handed. In September 1542, Juan Rodriguez Cabrillo discovered the Bay of San Diego. In 1602 Sebastian Vizcaino discovered the Bay of Monterey. Since the Spaniards saw no wealth, the most powerful incentive to settlement (and evangelization), they let 200 years pass after Cabrillo's visit before beginning settlement.

Missions and settlements in the Spanish province of Texas (not counting El Paso, Ysleta and Socorro) began almost 100 years after they were established in New Mexico. Concerned that the French would lay claim to the region now called East Texas, the Spaniards ordered Alonso de Leon and Fray Damian Massanet to start missions. On May 25, 1690, they founded San Francisco de Los Tejas. The following year another mission was established, but the threat of Indian attack and other adversity forced the Spaniards to abandon East Texas by 1693. Two decades later, six missions were started in the province, but the first to endure was San Antonio de Valero, at the site of the present city by that name in south-central Texas. Of more than twenty missions built at a cost of millions of pesos, only those in the areas of San Antonio and La Bahia survived until the nineteenth century.

Evangelization of lands now in Arizona began in the late 1690s, led by an intrepid Jesuit missionary named Eusebio Kino. Working among the Pima, Papago, Yuma and other Indians from 1687 until his death in 1711, he established twenty-nine missions, two of them in Arizona. These missions, like those in Texas, were under constant threat from hostile Indians.

The decision to evangelize and settle California was forced upon the Spaniards by political concerns. They feared that the Russians, pushing down from Alaska, would claim California. Thus on July 1, 1769, Mission San Diego was founded. Less than a year later, the presidio and mission at Monterey were going up. San Gabriel, San Luis Obispo, San Antonio, and San Carlos followed within four years. By 1776, the San Francisco mission was going up. In all, twenty-one missions were built in California, none of them more than a day's journey from the previous one.

The Spaniards also planted the cross and flag on lands now in the state of Washington. In 1774, a ship sailed through the strait of Juan de Fuca and into Puget Sound, where Fray Tomas de la Peña and Fray Juan Crespi celebrated Mass for the first time in that region. In July of 1775, the Spaniards began a small colony on the Olympic Peninsula.[1] Though apparently it no longer existed in 1800, the Spaniards claimed that territory until 1819 when it became part of the United States under the Adams-Onis Treaty.

THE MISSION PROCESS

Evangelization began with conquest; the Spaniards came to impose their civilization on the Indians. In their initial contacts in New Mexico, the Spaniards were quick to resort to violence. One of Coronado's lieutenants executed several hundred Tewa Indians because they refused to provide food for the expedition. In 1582, Antonio de Espejo, who had gone to New Mexico a year earlier to search for three missionaries, executed sixteen Indians and burned others at the stake for refusing to provide food.[2]

Oñate burned Acoma Pueblo in retaliation for the killing of thirteen Spaniards. In various expeditions to New Mexico, after the Pueblo revolt had expelled the Spaniards in 1680, Diego de Vargas set fire to several Indian villages. After the reoccupation of Santa Fe in 1693, he executed seventy of the Indian leaders.

The violence created terror. Alonso de Benavides, custodian of the New Mexico missions, wrote in 1634: "So great is the fear which God has instilled in them of these few Spaniards that they do not come near where they are."[3] It was in that context that evangelization was carried out.

When they first came to the New World, the Europeans thought the Indians had no religion. Then they saw their beliefs as idolatry, devil worship, or witchcraft. That view prevailed in New Mexico in the seventeenth century. Benavides theorized that "infinite superstition and idolatries, bloody sacrifices and devastating wars" had led many families to separate and that led to different languages among the Indians.[4]

The basic mission structure was the reduction, usually encompassing villages and surrounding cultivated areas where the Indians were obliged to live and work. The reductions were common in Florida, California, Arizona, and Texas. In New Mexico, where the missionaries dealt with sedentary peoples, they usually placed the mission compound within or just outside the pueblos. Within the reductions were farms or shops where the Indians were required to work. Another structure, inspired by the European feudal system, was the *encomienda*. In lieu of pay military officials were given the tribute or labor of a group of Indians, who enjoyed few of the fruits of their labor.

Needless to say, these structures violated human rights, even if slavery was not then considered wrong. Though initial entry was in many cases voluntary, the Indians were forced to work at various tasks in the mission compound, from building the churches to caring for livestock to cultivating the soil and raising the crops. Moreover, they had to give up their religion for Christianity.

Instruments of worship such as masks, prayer sticks and prayer feathers were confiscated. Indian places of worship, such as the *kivas* of the Pueblos, were destroyed or closed. Perhaps as a result of the Indian revolts, some tolerance was evident in the later colonial period. Corporal punishment such as flogging and prolonged kneeling was not uncommon. Native religious leaders who persisted in following their beliefs were whipped or executed. In 1675, San Juan Tewa leader Popé and forty-six other Indian leaders were publicly whipped in Santa Fe. Five years later Popé led the Pueblo Indian revolt.

At the same time that the missionaries gave instruction in Catholic dogma, they taught Spanish and demanded respect for Spanish law and authority. They preached the values of sedentary life while dealing with nomadic people. They also urged the Indians to accept the Spanish political system, social customs and dress codes, and to avoid drinking alcohol and using body paint. Indian women had to convert to Catholicism to have a legitimate marriage with a Spaniard. Taken together, the program of the missionaries sought to persuade the Indians to abandon not only their religion but their culture as well.

By the Spaniards' own accounts, many of the missions were a great success. In 1606, Bishop Juan Cabezas Altamirano, the first Catholic prelate to set foot on territories now in the United States, visited the missions in Florida. He was apparently impressed, because the missions were elevated to a custodia in 1609 and to a province of the Diocese of Cuba in 1612. By 1634, thirty-four Franciscans were in Florida ministering to 40,000 Indians. In 1655, seventy friars worked in thirty-eight missions from St. Augustine to Georgia and west to present-day Tallahassee. Nearly two decades later, in 1674, Bishop Gabriel de Calderon spent eight months visiting the missions. He conferred minor orders on seven young men and confirmed 13,152 persons.

The reports from New Mexico were even more impressive. By 1604 the missions in New Mexico had been declared a commissary, the basic organizational unit. By 1616, they had been elevated to custodia. In 1625 there were fourteen missionaries in the territory. That year the new custodian of the missions, Fray Alonso de Benavides, brought twelve more. The colony was divided into seven missionary districts. Churches and chapels were built in the various pueblos. In the larger ones there was a mission compound with workshops where the Indians were taught weaving, leatherwork, blacksmithing, and other skills. In

1630, Benavides wrote that 60,000 Pueblo Indians in ninety villages accepted the Catholic faith.

"All the Indians are now converted, baptized and well ministered to, with 33 convents and churches in the principal pueblos and more than 150 churches throughout the other pueblos," he reported. "Here where scarcely 30 years earlier all was idolatry and worship of the devil, without any vestige of civilization, today they worship our true God and Lord. The whole land is dotted with churches and convents and crosses along the road."[5]

Similarly, in California the Franciscans claimed to have converted 54,000 Indians during the sixty-five years that those missions were in operation. In economic terms, these missions were a remarkable success. In 1834, they were valued at $78 million.

The foregoing would give the impression that evangelization was accepted eagerly by the Indians. In fact, however, the number of willing converts was only a fraction of the statistics cited above. Half a century after Benavides's glowing report, in 1680, the Indians revolted, killing 380 settlers and twenty-one missionaries and forcing the survivors to retreat south of El Paso. The suppression of religious beliefs was one of the causes of the uprising. The Hopi and Zuni tribes endured half a century of coercive missionary work and forced labor. But eventually they killed the missionaries and returned to their ancient religious practices. The Hopi never again accepted the missioners. There were similar revolts in California and in Georgia, where the Guale took up arms because the missionaries forbade them to practice polygamy. Whether or not large numbers were converted, disease and forced labor decimated the Indian population. In New Mexico, according to one estimate, of 40,000 Indians who lived there before the Spaniards came, only 16,000 remained in 1680. In California, there were 72,000 Indians in 1769 and only 15,000 in 1836. Infant mortality was as high as 86 percent.[6] Some historians consider the figures for the initial population and of the surviving population of New Mexico in 1680 as serious underestimates. But there is no argument that there was a steep decline after the Spaniards came. In Florida, only a remnant of the Timucua and other tribes remained. They merged with the Seminole Indians, who moved down from Alabama and western Georgia. The decimation continued under

American rule. In the second Seminole War (1835-52) the majority were killed or forcibly removed to reservations in the West. Only 1,500 Seminoles lived in Florida by the late twentieth century.[7]

In Florida, the blame had to be shared by Spain, France, England, and the United States. It was a battleground from the time the Spaniards established themselves in 1565. In 1702 and 1704 the British and their Indian allies destroyed the Florida missions. By 1708 only St. Augustine remained,[8] and it was attacked repeatedly all during that half-century. The French held Pensacola from 1719 to 1723. The Treaty of Paris, signed in 1763, gave England sovereignty over Florida although it was returned to Spain in 1783. But much of what Spain had built there at such great effort had been abandoned twenty years earlier. In 1795 Spain sold West Florida, which included parts of Alabama and Mississippi, to France. Then in 1818 General Andrew Jackson invaded Pensacola. Spain finally ceded Florida to the United States in 1821.

In Texas, the missions failed not only because the Comanches and other nomadic tribes would not accept mission life but also because the Spaniards had to battle the French, who had expelled them from east Texas by 1719. In California, five years after the founding of the first mission, only 491 children had been baptized in all of upper California.

Lack of success has also been attributed to the failure to learn Indian languages. At first the missionaries made an effort, but as time went on, they became lax. When he visited the missions in New Mexico in 1760, Bishop Tamaron criticized the failure to learn Indian languages. A report in 1776 showed the language deficiency was widespread.[9] By 1817 no missionaries in New Mexico spoke Indian languages.[10]

Also, the missionaries were decimated on four occasions, in addition to the constant attrition due to the elements and Indian attacks. In 1767, the Jesuits were expelled from the Spanish empire. Caught in a struggle between the papacy and the Bourbon monarchs of Europe, the order had earlier been banned from Portugal and its colonies in 1759. It was dissolved by Pope Clement XIV in 1773 and not restored as a world order until 1814.[11] The missions principally affected in what is now the

United States were those in Arizona, permanently founded in 1731, two decades after Eusebio Kino's death. The Franciscans who replaced the Jesuits had to cover more territory. Chronologically, the second exodus occurred between 1793 and the 1830s, when the missions were secularized. The objective, to replace Franciscan missionaries with secular priests, was only partially achieved. As a consequence, many of the missions were abandoned. The third time a big loss of mission personnel occurred was after Mexico won its independence in 1821. Many of the clergy, being Spanish nationals, returned voluntarily to Spain. Others were expelled. On December 20, 1827, the Mexican government ordered the expulsion of Franciscans from New Mexico and Arizona, leaving many of the missions and settlements without priests.[12]

As time went on, it became clear that the early claims about the success of the missions had been vastly exaggerated. Christian duties were often performed under compulsion. Some practices were accepted out of love of ritual or ceremony, but few converts abandoned their old beliefs. During the eighteenth century, the Pueblo religious leaders returned to their kivas to worship in the old ways. After 200 years the Pueblo Indians, those most susceptible to evangelization because of their sedentary ways, conformed to Christianity only superficially.[13]

There were, however, some success stories. The Papagos retained their Christianity even though they had no priests. The faith also endured in the Tewa Indians who had fled New Mexico with the retreating survivors of the Pueblo Revolt in 1680 and settled in El Paso. Assimilated Indians in San Antonio and other places also remained Catholic.

Overall, however, the statistics do not proclaim the missions a great success. In upper New Mexico, the missions served an Indian population of 12,000 in 1750; by 1800 the numbers dropped to 10,000 and remained at that level. In the meantime, the number of settlements of the colonists had increased to 102. In California, escape from the missions was common. In Texas, most of the Indians had fled the missions by 1813. The California missions were ruined by secularization, which began in 1834. Under that process, the administration of the missions was transferred from the Franciscans to secular clergy and the mission lands were parceled out to those who worked them.[14] By the outbreak of the Mexican War in 1846, most of the missions had not only lost their clergy but had nearly been destroyed.[15]

The Spaniards were less successful at creating a church in the sense of a "people of God" than they were at creating church structures. Their society in the northern provinces was rife with divisions. In New Spain there were seven castes: *gachupines*, born in Spain; *creoles*, Spaniards born in the New World; *mestizos*, a mix of whites and Indians; *mulattos*, a blend of whites and blacks; *zambos*, an intermingling of blacks and Indians; and finally, pure blacks and Indians. The prejudice against the Indians, by missioner and colonist alike, was unrelenting. Missioners commonly compared Indians to children, inferior and incapable of change. They were accused of "congenital idleness, a natural repugnance for work."[16] In 1845, Fray Narcisco Duran wrote that the Indians needed a slave driver rather than a missioner.

Slave, indeed, was the most apt description for the role of most Indians. In New Mexico in the seventeenth century, the missioners and the royal governors alike, locked in a struggle for power, exploited the Indians. The governors established workshops where Indian slaves captured in raids produced textiles and other goods then sold to enrich their master. But the missions similarly forced the Indians to work in their workshops or fields. One governor by the name of Mendizabal (1659-1669) was convicted for using slave labor to enrich himself.[17] But many others went unpunished. The ill-treatment extended to the lower castes of mixed race, the mestizos, and the zambos, and persons of black and Indian ancestry.

ORGANIZATION OF THE SECULAR CHURCH

In the Southwest and West, the missions were directed by the Franciscans headquartered in Mexico (except for Arizona, administered by the Jesuits until 1767). The Colegio de La Santa Cruz de Queretaro, built in the 1680s, provided the missionaries for Texas and, later, for Arizona; the Colegio de San Fernando el Grande, for California and, briefly, for Texas; the Provincia del Santo Evangelio, for El Paso and New Mexico; and the Colegio de Guadalupe de Zacatecas, for Texas and, later, California. The Franciscan colleges were founded to carry out the work of the Congregation for the Propagation of the Faith, created by Pope Gregory XV in 1622.

These northern colonial provinces were also under the jurisdiction of dioceses in Mexico. Initially, New Mexico was nominally under the Diocese of Guadalajara. After 1621, it became part of the newly created Diocese of Durango. The Diocese of Linares, created in 1777 and later renamed Monterey or Nuevo Leon, received jurisdiction over Texas, previously under the Diocese of Guadalajara. The Diocese of Sonora, whose first bishop arrived in 1783, included Arizona and California. The bishops rarely visited their far-off provinces. New Mexico received episcopal visits only three times in the eighteenth century.[18] During one period, a bishop did not appear for seventy years. No bishop set foot in Texas or Arizona during the Mexican period (1821-1836 in Texas, 1821-1846 in Arizona).[19] Yet, in New Mexico at least, the rarity of episcopal visits is not necessarily evidence of neglect, as charged by some historians, because from 1730 on the bishop had a vicar representing him in Santa Fe. Moreover, the Franciscans resisted the bishop's jurisdiction in New Mexico.

Until 1798, parishes directed by secular priests did not exist in New Mexico. In the Province of Texas during the eighteenth century, two parishes came into being, in San Antonio and in La Bahia. The bishop of Durango recommended in 1767 that four of New Mexico's Franciscan posts be turned over to priests from the diocese. These were the Spanish towns of Santa Fe, Santa Cruz de la Cañada, Albuquerque, and El Paso.[20] The change was desirable, in the bishop's view, because these settlements were populated by colonists rather than Indians. The recommendation, however, was not implemented for decades.

In the background was a struggle for power. The bishop wanted to extend his authority over the Church in New Mexico. The Franciscans, however, resisted the change. Nevertheless, by 1820 these towns were being served by five secular priests. After Mexican independence, officials of the Diocese of Durango ordered the secularization of five more missions. In 1840, the last friars in New Mexico died. A symbolic Franciscan presence returned when the bishop of Durango sent Fray Mariano de

Jesús López in 1845. He served among the Zuni, Laguna, and Acoma Indians until his death in 1848. No other Franciscan joined him.[21] Secular clergy increased to eight in 1829 and eleven in 1846.

In California there were no secular priests in 1840 and only five in 1846. Two secular priests served in Texas in 1836, none in Arizona in 1846.[22] The Franciscans, who depended on Spain for their vocations, did not develop local structures. More than 100 years elapsed after Juan de Oñate established the first missions before the area could claim its first priest. He was Santiago de Roybal, ordained about 1728 by the bishop of Durango. He was the first native secular priest in the Southwest. Apparently the Franciscans did not ordain any native New Mexicans. Fray Angelico Chavez, a twentieth century historian, claimed to be the first native Franciscan since the reconquest of New Mexico in 1693.[23]

Nevertheless, vocations were there awaiting a man of vision to develop them. Unfortunately, New Mexico would have the opportunity to develop its own clergy for only a brief time. When Bishop Jose Antonio Laureano de Zubiría made his first visit to New Mexico in 1833, a priest named António José Martinez offered to establish a preparatory school for seminarians. About thirty students studied at the school and sixteen were eventually ordained to the priesthood, most of them by Bishop Zubiría and four by French Bishop Jean Lamy, the first prelate of the Diocese of New Mexico.[24] Lamy and his successors, however, showed little interest in Hispanic priestly vocations, looking instead to Europe, particularly France, to provide them. A few native vocations to the priesthood also developed in Texas in the 1790s and early 1800s.

The Church developed slowly in New Mexico because of the failure to establish a diocese. As early as 1630, Fray de Benavides had asked the pope to establish one in New Mexico. The next requests came from the Spanish Cortes in 1818, from the Mexican Congress in 1823, and again in 1830. The closest New Mexico came to having adequate episcopal care was in the waning days of the Mexican period. In 1831 Zubiría was ordained bishop of Durango. He made three pastoral visits to New Mexico, 1833, 1845, and 1850. After the first visit he bestowed on

Father Juan Felipe Ortiz, a native New Mexican from Santa Fe, the power to administer the sacrament of confirmation. Padre Martinez was also given authority to confirm.

In 1840, at the request of the Mexican government, the Vatican established a diocese for the upper and lower Californias. The bishop, Francisco García Diego y Moreno, was consecrated the same year but did not arrive in Santa Barbara, the seat of the new diocese, until nearly the end of 1841. He had difficulties recruiting clergy in Mexico and thus was not able to organize the diocese properly. There were then only seventeen Franciscans in upper California. But he did recruit seminarians in Mexico and ordained six of them during his brief administration. Already 55 when he became bishop, he died six years later in 1846.

In New Mexico and Texas, dioceses would not be created until those territories were lost to Mexico. Three years after Texas won its independence, the pope severed that territory from its Mexican diocese and made it a prefecture, appointing John L. Odin as vice-prefect apostolic. In 1842, Odin was consecrated bishop and in 1847 Texas became a diocese.

Nevertheless, in most of the Southwest, a secular church was slowly developing in the 1800s. Though missions had declined, the mestizo settlements had grown steadily. By the 1820s they were often served by secular clergy, some of them indigenous, particularly in New Mexico and Texas. Though historians ignored that church or spoke negatively of its presence, it thrived during trying times in New Mexico, El Paso, and the lower Rio Grande region of Texas and made an important beginning in California in the 1840s.[25]

THE CHURCH OF THE POOR

The Spaniards succeeded in creating a new people. Amidst extremes of climate, attacks by hostile tribes and the struggle demanded by a harsh land, the mestizos flourished. These people, often with only a few priests, developed a self-reliant religion. It is to them, for the most part hardly literate peasants, that the faith owes its existence in the Southwest.

When the missioners were removed or died out, it was they

who carried on. They were sustained by beliefs, rituals, and practices that one day would be disparaged as superstition by those bishops and clergy unable to recognize their true value.

In New Mexico, the piety of the mestizos was dominated by the "spiritual and material images of their crucified Nazarene and the queenly virgin."[26] They were inclined to a strong penitential spirit, a Spanish legacy, evident from the beginning of settlement. Juan de Oñate, for example, scourged himself. In New Mexico, they organized as the *Fraternidad Piadosa de Nuestro Padre Jesus Nazareno*, commonly known as the *Penitentes*. Their origin is unknown, though some scholars say it can be traced back to the Third Order of St. Francis, a lay branch of the Franciscans in existence during the Spanish period.

With priests frequently absent, the *Penitentes* led their communities in the observance of the feasts of the liturgical calendar. For Lent and Holy Week they had elaborate penitential rituals, reenacting the crucifixion, leading the congregation in the rosary and in reciting the stations of the cross. When someone died, they led the burial prayers. They also taught Christian doctrine to the young, provided material assistance to those in need, and mediated disputes among families. "It would not be an exaggeration to say that these *Penitentes* assured the survival of the Catholic faith in New Mexico during the Mexican period and beyond," wrote the priest who was chaplain of the *Penitentes* in 1988.[27]

Bishop Zubiría regarded the penitential practices of the *Penitentes* as excessive. His successors tried to control their devotions; failing, they denied sacraments or ministry to its members. But since they had the support of the people, the *Penitentes* endured. There was a partial restoration in 1947. Archbishop Edwin V. Byrne formally recognized "the Brothers of Jesus of Nazareth (commonly called the *Penitentes*)" as a pious Catholic society and agreed to guide the Brotherhood himself.[28] However, not until 1974, when Roberto Sanchez was ordained the first native Hispanic archbishop of the Archdiocese of Santa Fe, were the *Penitentes* fully reconciled.

To this day in the remote villages of New Mexico, still visited only rarely by clergy, the faith of the people reveals the self-reliance, strong religious life, and devotion built by the *Penitentes*.

PART II

American Conquest and the Melting-Pot Church

—3—

A New Conquest
(1848–1890)

Early in the nineteenth century, a new conquest started in the Southwest. North American trappers and traders began to enter New Mexico. Clipper ships began to visit ports in California. Settlers began moving into Texas. Under the Spanish policy of closed borders, these visitors were seen as interlopers and expelled. But when Mexico won its independence, they were welcomed. The Mexican government gave Stephen Austin and 300 North American families a grant in Texas. In New Mexico, some trappers bought large tracts of land, a policy criticized by Father Antonio José Martínez. He also denounced the exploitation of the Indians by the North Americans.[1] North Americans also settled in California, marrying the daughters of some of the leading citizens. These settlers turned out to be the vanguard of an invasion.

In the mid-1830s, the North American settlers in Texas revolted. By 1836, they had defeated Mexico's army and proclaimed their independence. In the meantime, Anglo Americans in other parts of the Southwest were helping to condition public opinion in the United States to seize the rest of those territories. They sent back highly unfavorable reports about the Hispanic inhabitants of the Southwest.

The cause of the conflict was "lust for seizure."[2] The administration of President James A. Polk decided to annex California. First Polk tried to bribe Mexican officials; then he tried to start a revolution. Next he attempted to compel Mexico to sell California. When all that failed, the United States declared war. The purpose of the invasion was not only to seize the coveted territory but to humiliate Mexico. One army marched through New Mexico, Arizona, and California. Another crossed the Rio Grande at Matamoros, Eagle Pass, and El Paso. Ultimately, a third one landed at Veracruz and, following the invasion route of Hernán Cortez, captured Mexico City in 1847.

The invaders committed many crimes. Some of the soldiers raped mothers and daughters in the presence of their husbands and fathers.[3] They also desecrated churches. General Zachary Taylor, commanding one of the armies, collected $1 million from the Mexican people by force of arms. As a consequence of such acts, bitterness endured for generations.

The United States annexed half of Mexico's territory, including Texas, whose independence had not been recognized by Mexico but which the United States had admitted as a state in 1845. These territories contained, in addition to 180,000 to 250,000 Indians, between 75,000 and 100,000 inhabitants with at least partial Hispanic heritage. Most of them, about 60,000, lived in New Mexico. Of the remainder, about 8,000 lived in California, 2,000 in Arizona and the rest of them in Texas. Through the Treaty of Guadalupe Hidalgo, signed in 1848, they became citizens of the United States, with specific guarantees of their civil rights and land titles. It soon became evident, however, that the provisions of the treaty would not be honored.

Anglo Americans refused to accept the Hispanics as equals. Many agreed with the political philosopher John C. Calhoun that only the "free white race" should be added to the union.[4]

Many also agreed with Anglo Americans in California who were willing to allow non-whites to live there "but only if they had few or no human rights and if they could be considered without argument to be born inferior."[5] As a result of these views, Hispanics suffered violence whose exact toll will never be known. But between 1865 and 1920, according to estimates, more Mexicans were lynched in the Southwest than blacks in the old South.[6]

The violence was so intense and widespread in some areas as to give the impression that the white race was crushing out the inferior race and that the Mexicans were doomed. In California, 2,000 miners attacked a foothills town inhabited by Mexicans, Chileans, and Peruvians, killing scores. Elsewhere, persons were hanged on the basis of unsubstantiated accusations or for misdemeanors. A man was lynched for getting into a fist fight, a woman for killing a miner who broke into her house, a man for refusing to play the fiddle for a group of Anglo Texans.

Historian Walter Prescott Webb wrote that one law applied to Mexicans and another, less rigorous, to political leaders and prominent Americans.[7] In west Texas, Judge Roy Bean could find nothing in the law that made killing a Mexican a crime. Writing about that period, a novelist said: "Anglo children who once had been taught to think that Indians were not human were now raised to think that Mexicans were even less so."[8]

Besides physical violence, Hispanics suffered what later came to be called "institutional violence." In the courts, they were sometimes disqualified from being witnesses because they were not white. Through legal and illegal means, they were denied the right to vote. Squatters who seized their lands were not prosecuted; neither were persons who assaulted them. But if the victims defended themselves, they were punished severely. Real estate taxes were raised until Hispanic owners lost their properties for being delinquent; then the rates were lowered for the new Anglo American owners. Others were dispossessed by means of a statute that required validation of all land titles issued by Mexico. In California, a "foreign miners' tax" was imposed on Hispanics who had become citizens through the Treaty of Guadalupe Hidalgo. As time passed, Hispanics were excluded from all but menial jobs, receiving no opportunity to develop new skills.

In economic terms, the effect of the physical and institutional violence was to impoverish Hispanics as a people. During colonial and Mexican times, society had consisted of a small upper class of persons in top government positions, the officers in the army, the ranchers and large land owners. Beneath them were the majority of the settlers—artisans, cowboys, foremen on the ranches, craftsmen and tradesmen in the settlements. The Indians were the lowest class of workers.[9] The Anglo American conquest reduced many to the lowest level. Only where Hispanics were the majority or a high proportion of the population, as in New Mexico, El Paso, and San Antonio, were they able to retain strong political and economic influence. Whereas Hispanics as a people once owned countless horses, vast herds of sheep, and lands stretching to distant horizons, within two or three decades they found themselves on reduced acreage or holding only the poorest lands. Judge Don Pablo de la Guerra, one of the authors of the California Constitution, said in a speech before the legislature: "I have seen old men of sixty and seventy years of age weeping because they have been cast out of their ancestral home. They have been humiliated and insulted. They have been refused the privilege of cutting their own firewood."[10]

As another effect of the conquest, Hispanics were branded as a criminal population. Since the authorities would not protect them, they had to take the law into their own hands when attacked or dispossessed. They were then hunted down as bandits. In fact, many of these men were guerrilla fighters taking the only option available to them. Tiburcio Vasquez, one of those caught and hanged, said he had only tried to avenge Yankee injustices committed against his people. "I believe we were being unjustly deprived of the social rights that belonged to us," he said.[11] Today, historians and sociologists, both Anglo and Hispano, are likely to see these incidents of "banditry" as justified retaliation rather than crime.[12]

Violence and discrimination forced many ordinary people as well as leaders to emigrate to Mexico. One of the heroes of the Texas Revolution, Captain Juan Seguin, later the mayor of San Antonio, was one of those exiles. "I had to leave Texas, abandon all, for which I had fought and spent my fortune, to become a wanderer."[13]

The worst effect, however, was a complex of defeatism — apathy, apparent indifference, passivity, and lack of motivation — that continued to affect many Hispanics into the twentieth century. The people felt that no matter what they did, they would remain on the periphery of the economic, political, and social systems.

The absolute subjugation of the Hispanic population became possible because Anglo Americans controlled the armed forces, the police, the courts, the legislatures, and the economy. The discovery of gold in California nine days after the signing of the Treaty of Guadalupe Hidalgo in 1848 brought so many settlers that in a year they outnumbered the Mexicans ten to one. By 1850, California had 380,000 inhabitants, only 15 percent of them Hispanics, a proportion that continued to decline. Between 1851 and 1860, only 4,302 entered the state. By 1870, those of Spanish origin accounted for only four percent of the population. Between 1851 and 1900, they constituted less than one percent of the immigrants to California.[14] Low immigration was due to the extreme violence and discrimination which Hispanics experienced in California during that period.

In Texas, Anglo Americans moved in so fast during the 1820s and 1830s that by 1836, when the territory declared itself a republic, they numbered 30,000, with only 5,000 Mexicans. In 1846, the population had gone up to 140,000, with very little of that increase consisting of Hispanics.[15] Only in New Mexico did the Hispanics remain in the majority until the 20th century.

Beginning in the 1880s, Hispanics in the Southwest obtained a reprieve from the categorical rejection they had suffered in most areas since 1846. Now, they were welcome and even recruited—but only as cheap labor in a few industries, among them agriculture, the railroads, and mining. Workers were recruited not only in the Mexican American barrios but also in Mexico itself. The new policy could be traced to a number of developments. In 1882, Congress passed the Chinese Exclusion Act, which halted immigration from that country. A few years later a similar agreement curtailed immigration from Japan. In the 1920s, new laws excluded Eastern Europeans. As a result, Mexicans and Mexican Americans were in great demand for menial labor. They were chosen because they were docile, hardworking, and easy to "send home" when they were no longer needed. They were simply transported to the Mexican border.

At the same time, irrigation opened millions of acres for growing fruits and vegetables. The completion of the first transcontinental railroad in 1869 and the development of refrigerated railroad cars in 1887 made it possible to ship the produce to the populated centers of the East. Passage of a tariff on the importation of sugar facilitated the growth of the sugar beet industry, which required much hand labor.

Thus Hispanics were finally assigned a place in Anglo American society, even if temporary and provisional. They were welcome only if and when the labor for which they were designated was available. They were not considered equals to Anglo Americans, not welcome to associate socially with them, and not permitted to advance themselves economically, politically, and socially.

FOREIGN SHEPHERDS

Before the Mexican War, only one diocese and one vicariate had headquarters in the Southwest. The diocese for upper and lower California had been established in 1840, but the first bishop had not arrived until 1841. The same year Texas had been made a missionary vicariate subject to Rome. Dioceses were created rapidly following the change in sovereignty from Mexico to the United States. The Diocese of Galveston (Texas) was created in 1847; Santa Fe (New Mexico), in 1853; San Francisco, 1853; Sacramento (Grass Valley), in 1868; San Antonio, 1874; Denver, 1887; Dallas, 1890; and Tucson, 1897.

With two exceptions, the first bishops of the dioceses in New Mexico, Arizona, Colorado, and Texas were Frenchmen. The first prelate of San Antonio was an American of Minorcan (Spanish) descent and the first in Dallas was an Irishman, Thomas Brennan. The first bishops of the dioceses of San Francisco and Los Angeles were Spanish, but an Irishman, Bishop Eugene O'Connell, was chosen for Sacramento. The Vicariate Apostolic of Brownsville was created in 1874 with another American of Minorcan descent as bishop.

These bishops, all but one born in Europe, attempted to create a church like the one they had left. The one who perhaps tried the hardest was Jean Baptiste Lamy, the first bishop of New Mexico. He boasted that he was creating a little Auvergne, the name of his province in France. Even the architectural style of the cathedral he started in Santa Fe was French, as were the artisans he brought to build it.

Lamy was particularly concerned with ecclesiastical buildings: churches, chapels, schools, and hospitals. He was successful. Fifteen years after his arrival, he reported to the Holy See that he

had built forty-five churches and chapels and had repaired eight-
een or twenty old ones. Moreover, he had established four
houses of the Sisters of Loretto and three of Christian Brothers.
Lamy also established a seminary, but it lasted only a few years.
Nevertheless, native New Mexicans who studied there were
eventually ordained: José Samuel García and Manuel Ribera.
Lamy did ordain four other natives between 1856 and 1859:
Ramon Medina, Miguel Vigil, Manuel Chavez and Sembran
Tafoya.[16] But in general he preferred to staff the diocese and
later archdiocese with Frenchmen. He or his associates made
several trips to Europe to recruit both priests and Brothers and
to Kentucky and Ohio to recruit Sisters.

Lamy and his associate, Joseph P. Machebeuf, later the first
bishop of Denver, have been credited with bringing Gallic discipline to the church in New Mexico. But he also caused division
that took generations to reconcile. The Council of Baltimore
had appointed Lamy to head the Vicariate of New Mexico *in
partibus infidelium* (in the region of the infidels), a fixed phrase
for any missionary territory. The designation was perhaps justified in Texas, considering how many indigenous peoples were
not yet converted. But it was clearly an affront to the Catholicism that had existed in New Mexico for 250 years. The biased
view of the American church and of the bishops sent to the
Southwest was that there had been a glorious period of evangelization by the missionaries from Spain and an almost total
collapse of the church during the Mexican period. Perhaps that
explains why Lamy's relations with the native clergy were poor.
At one point, he expressed the intent "to keep them under fear"
and on one occasion he wrote to the bishop of Cincinnati: "I
must be patient and catch them doing wrong. I suspended one
of the senior clerics; perhaps that will be an example for the
others."[17] Perhaps his hostility was due in part to the uncere-
monious reception he received when he arrived in Santa Fe. Not
having received notification of the creation of the vicariate and
the appointment of Lamy, the New Mexican clergy would not
accept him without credentials signed by their bishop. They suggested he see Bishop Zubiria in Durango. Lamy therefore had
to journey 800 miles on horseback to get the necessary papers.

There were sixteen priests in the vicariate of New Mexico

when Lamy arrived but seven of them were old and sickly. Of the nine remaining, Lamy removed five, including the ones most respected by the people. The most famous was Antonio José Martínez, the pastor of Taos, who had been the person most responsible for building a native clergy. By failing to develop an effective seminary and relying so heavily on European clergy and religious, Lamy killed the tradition of priesthood that had begun to develop during the Mexican period. It would be generations and five French bishops later before an Anglo American bishop would try to revive it.

TEXAS

Though the first bishops in Texas were also French, the church they encountered was different from that of New Mexico in one significant respect. In New Mexico, the majority of the inhabitants were Hispanics and it would remain so until almost mid-twentieth century. But in Texas, the Mexican Americans were a minority of the population. Immigrants were arriving so fast from Germany, Czechoslovakia, France, and Poland that Father John Timon who was named prefect apostolic of Texas in 1839 could entertain the notion that these immigrants would be the primary flock. At least a few priests preferred to serve the immigrants rather than the Mexicans. Father Florent Vandenberghe tried to persuade the Jesuits to take responsibility for Brownsville so that he could work among "civilized people" in Louisiana or North Texas.[18] When Father Dominic Manucy was appointed to head the new Vicariate Apostolic of Brownsville, he responded with a letter saying: "I consider this appointment as Vicar Apostolic of Brownsville the worst sentence that could have been given me for any crime. The Catholic population is composed almost exclusively of Mexican greasers — cattle drovers and thieves. No money can be got out of these people, not even to bury their fathers."[19]

The attitudes of Jean M. Odin, the first bishop of the Diocese of Galveston (encompassing all of Texas), toward Mexicans are not clear. He made great efforts to recruit priests in Europe for these immigrant groups. He also brought three Spaniards to work along the San Antonio River and left them there throughout the 1840s. Then and subsequently in some areas, classes were taught in Spanish and foreign clergy learned Spanish instead of English and served Hispanics all their lives. But in 1840, he removed the only two native priests above the Nueces Valley. As one of the French priests put it bluntly, the way to make progress was to replace the Mexican clergy with foreigners.[20] The issue was not so much ministry as it was who was to provide it. There the early bishops of Texas showed a decided preference for Europeans over natives.

The bishops of Texas built institutions but the work was slow. In 1849, there were only twelve priests in all of Texas to serve 20,000 Catholics. By 1860 there were only 42 churches and 44 chapels in the state. They were hardly adequate for the burgeoning population. In rural areas, four priests served 80,000 people. Like Lamy, the French bishops recruited religious congregations and orders to come to Texas: the Oblates of Mary Immaculate, the Sisters of the Incarnate Word, and other groups from Europe. But though each of the Sisters' congregations found several native vocations, the clergy did not find candidates for the priesthood. The progress reports tell of the completion of churches, chapels, schools, colleges, and hospitals, but not seminaries. They could not seem to get them off the ground. Mexico could not have provided any priests if the Texas bishops requested them; many Spaniards had returned home when Mexico won its independence. But when twenty-two Sisters of Charity, forced to leave Mexico because of church-state conflicts at the time,[21] arrived in Brownsville in 1875, Manucy refused to accept them. Like Lamy, the bishops of Texas went to Europe again and again to find most of their clergy and religious.

Some clergy thought the primary beneficiaries of these church institutions and of the clergy and religious brought from Europe ought to be the dominant English-speaking population. For example, an Oblate priest in Brownsville thought St. Joseph College should cater to the governing class.[22] Due to lack of resources, not goodwill, the Sisters of Charity of the Incarnate Word in their early years in Texas concentrated their efforts on non-Hispanic people. Schools they opened for Mexican American children often had to be closed. The Sisters of the Incarnate Word and Blessed Sacrament, however, established themselves first in the heavily Hispanic settlements of Brownsville and Corpus Christi.

In Texas and New Mexico, the European clergy did not understand some aspects of Hispanic piety. Father Timon marveled at how Hispanics were ready to die for their religion but hardly knew what it was about. In the wake of Protestant challenge, knowledge of the faith had become of paramount importance. But for heirs of an austere Iberian spirituality who had been living in isolation for a long time and had experienced neither the Protestant Reformation nor the Catholic Counter-Reformation, it was not what one knew but how one lived that made all the difference.

CALIFORNIA

When Bishop Diego y Moreno died in 1846, the embryonic institutional Mexican American church began to die as well. He had established Our Lady of Guadalupe Seminary, near Santa Ines Mission, in 1844. By the end of the following year, it had thirty-three students, though only a few were considered serious candidates for the priesthood. The seminary made it a policy to admit as many poor students as its resources would permit. After the bishop died, the seminary could not get the support it needed and, though it continued for seventeen years, apparently no native Mexican American priests were ordained. Almost a century would pass in southern California before there would be another diocesan seminary: St. John Seminary, founded in 1939 in Camarillo. Things moved faster in the north, where Hispanics were a tiny minority; St. Patrick's Seminary was established in Menlo Park in 1898.

The Catholic Church as institution grew rapidly in the years following Anglo American occupation. In 1851, a newspaper article boasted that "in almost every portion of the state, churches are erected, charitable and literary institutions are being founded and with the blessing of God we hope in a short time that California will shine forth a bright spot on the map of the Catholic Church."[23] As previously mentioned, the first See, called the Diocese of Monterey, had split in two by the early 1850s, creating the Archdiocese of San Francisco. In the 1860s, the Diocese of Grass Valley, later changed to Sacramento, was established.

Before he died Bishop Garcia Diego y Moreno had named a fellow Franciscan, Father José Gonzales Rubio, a Mexican, as his vicar general. Rubio guided the far-flung diocese until 1850, when a Spanish Dominican, Joseph Sadoc Alemany was appointed bishop. In 1853 Alemany was promoted to head the new Archdiocese of San Francisco and Thaddeus Amat, another Spaniard, succeeded him at Monterey. But in less than fifty years, the bishops of California would all be Irish. The first was the aforementioned Eugene O'Connell, the first bishop of Sacramento, who was succeeded by another Irishman, Patrick Manogue, in 1884. Alemany, who served in San Francisco until 1884, was followed by Archbishop Patrick Riordan. Amat, who died in 1878, was succeeded by another Spaniard, Bishop Francis Mora. But when he resigned in 1896, Bishop George Montgomery took over. Irish domination of the California hierarchy was now complete.

California had only sixteen priests (eleven Franciscans and five secular clergy) when it was occupied by the United States. When Father Gonzales Rubio saw the tide of immigrants arrive following the discovery of gold, he recruited priests in France and Oregon. Thanks to the generous response he received, especially from Oregon Archbishop Norbert Blanchet, he had twenty-eight priests when Alemany arrived a few years later. Alemany, who heard the news of his appointment while attending a general chapter of his order in Rome, recruited more priests in France, England, Ireland, and brought one from Spain.

The best response to these recruiting efforts came from Ireland. According to the San Francisco Archdiocesan Directory, of the 231 priests who served there from 1848 to 1904, exactly 146 or 63.2 percent were trained in Ireland. Only four priests, less than two percent, were trained in Spain and none was trained in Mexico. A survey of the religious orders showed the same pattern.[24]

In contrast to the growth of Irish clergy, the number of Hispanic priests steadily declined. When Alemany arrived, there were eleven Mexican priests in California. By 1856, there were four fewer; two had died and the other two had returned to Mexico.

THE CHRISTIAN EXPERIENCE OF THE POOR

Alemany, who was generally well-disposed toward the Mexicans, was concerned about the lack of Hispanic priests. He therefore asked for and received permission to establish a Franciscan novitiate and seminary, the Apostolic College of Our Lady of Sorrows. But Amat did not share his countryman's sympathies. He became embroiled in a dispute with the Franciscans and tried to force them to leave the college and minister to Indians at Mission San Luis Rey. Rome eventually ruled in favor of the Franciscans, but then Amat cancelled their faculties. Though they were restored three years later, the college languished until it was closed in 1900.

Throughout this period Hispanic influence steadily declined. In 1848, Archbishop John Hughes of New York took the trouble to write to José de La Guerra, a leading Catholic layman in California, to ask him about the condition of the Church. The Californian urged that an Hispanic be named to head it and added: "I think that at least it is indispensable that the bishop or bishops who are appointed be proficient in Spanish."[25] Alemany seemed to have the same concern, for he appointed Gonzales Rubio as his vicar. While Alemany was the bishop of Monterey, there was better sensitivity to the multi-cultural nature of the California church. For example, one of eighteen decrees approved by an assembly of the clergy said that couples getting married had a right to choose a priest from their own ethnic group to officiate at the ceremony.

Amat, however, was much less sympathetic to the Hispanics. In addition to his dispute with the Franciscans—or perhaps because of it—he removed Gonzales Rubio from his post as vicar general. The priest spent his remaining years, until his death in 1875, trying to save the Franciscan novitiate.

As Hispanics became a smaller proportion of the population in Texas and California, their culture and traditions as well as their persons came under increasing attack. In Arizona in the 1890s, for example, some municipalities passed ordinances banning Mexican fiestas. Amat published a pastoral letter critical of Mexican American religious practices. The bishop, one historian judged later, was afraid that the public processions and private devotions of the Hispanics would stir anti-Catholic feelings among the Protestants.[26] This same concern caused, at least in part, the continuing dispute with the *Penitentes* in New Mexico, whose activities were considered "contrary to modern ecclesiastical order and harmful to the image of Catholicism in the eyes of newcomers from the East."[27] Lamy found support in his desire to ban some of their practices in the "outspoken hostility of anti-Catholic civil leaders in the territory."[28]

Lamy tried without success to impose the rules of the Third Order of St. Francis. Then he started a policy of verifying, during administration of the sacraments, whether the recipient was a *Penitente*. If he was and refused to renounce membership, he was denied the sacrament. Lamy's directive was not carried out by some of the priests. When the bishop went on to deny the *Penitentes* the status of a religious society, they were incorporated as a benevolent society by the territorial legislature.

Jean Baptiste Salpointe, who succeeded Lamy, made further efforts to ban the *Penitentes*. He ordered pastors to deny the sacraments to those who insisted on observing traditional wakes. The order could not be enforced in isolated villages without priests. Even in the twentieth century, when someone died in the rural areas, the *Penitentes* had to lead the wake, dig the grave, and conduct the burial service. Many priests, therefore, did not enforce the rule. The Jesuits, in particular, did not cooperate, and for that reason, Salpointe forced them to leave New Mexico.[29]

The *Penitentes* in New Mexico represented what today would be called a parallel church that operated in rural areas where the official church had limited contact. Though their secrecy (another of the objections raised against them) and their penances may have seemed excessive to the newcomers from the East, the *Penitentes* provided structure to the church where there was no clergy. Yet the ecclesial authorities caused unnecessary alienation by trying to ban the brotherhoods. Fortunately, most people still filled the churches and chapels when priests were available and, at the same time, continued their traditional religious practices. Some people simply limited their contact with the church to those occasions that were absolutely essential: baptisms, marriages, and funerals. In Taos and in the San Luis Valley in Colorado, Presbyterians gained many converts. One historian wrote: "Many *Penitentes,* feeling rejected by the church of their forebears, converted to Presbyterianism. Some went on to become lay or ordained ministers."[30] Alienation was also caused by failure of the bishops and clergy to defend Hispanics. During this era, there was much violence against Hispanics; lynchings for little or no reason were common throughout the Southwest. If bishops and clergy spoke out in defense of the victims, no record was kept. More likely, they remained silent out of concern for being accepted by secular society. This was not an era when the church distinguished itself in its defense of the oppressed.

As in civil society, a process of conquest occurred in the church. The new leaders imposed their authority by displacing the previous leaders of the community. In New Mexico, Lamy excommunicated the most brilliant pastor: Padre Antonio José Martínez. Born in 1793 in Abiquiu, he was a descendant of one of the settlers who had come with Juan de Oñate in 1598. He was married at the age of nineteen but his wife died a year later in childbirth. The child, a daughter, survived only to die at the age of twelve. Four years after he became a widower, at the age of 24, Martínez entered the seminary in Durango. He was ordained on February 10, 1822, at the age of 29, by Bishop Juan Francisco de Castanizo. He returned to New Mexico in 1823 and served at Tome Pueblo and later at Taos, where he became the pastor in 1826.

Martínez distinguished himself not just by his efforts "to become a true minister of Christ,"[31] but by his interest in education. He started a co-educational school, an idea unheard-of at that time, and also a school to train seminarians. Among the many young men he propelled toward the priesthood was another talented New Mexican who was removed by Lamy, José Manuel Gallegos. In 1846, when the United States seized the territory, Martínez was 53 years old.

Martínez served as a member of the New Mexico legislature during the Mexican period and also during the early years of the North American administration. His involvement in politics, however, went much deeper. In 1847 when Indians and Hispanics revolted in Taos and killed the American governor, the plan was reportedly made in the home of Vicar Juan Felipe Ortiz with Martínez and another priest in attendance. The revolt was crushed and Martínez's alleged complicity was never proved. Nevertheless, he was the man the North Americans feared most.

When Martínez was 64 years old, Lamy excommunicated him "for grave and scandalous faults, his writings against due order and discipline in the Church."[32] The immediate cause of his expulsion was Martínez's opposition to the collection of tithes, as demanded by the bishop. But beneath the surface was a conflict that has occurred again and again between Hispanics and their European and North American bishops. In one sense it is based on differences in piety and culture; in another it is a struggle for self-determination by a people who have had only a peripheral role in the church since 1850.

Martínez refused to obey the excommunication order and continued to serve as a priest and to celebrate Mass in his private chapel for a few followers. Gallegos was removed from San Felipe parish in Albuquerque. Lamy accused him of being absent without leave from his parish and of living scandalously. The real reason, a New Mexico priest believed, was that the new French leadership wanted control of the most prosperous parishes.[33] After his suspension, Gallegos, who was respected by the people, was elected as a territorial delegate to Congress. Vicar Ortiz was also removed and replaced with a Frenchman.

Though some prominent laymen supported the French bishop, others opposed him. One sent a petition to Rome asking that Lamy be removed and replaced with Martínez. The Frenchmen, however, could do little about laymen directing religious ceremonies in remote villages without their knowledge and permission. They were never numerous enough or powerful enough to stop the *Penitentes*.

The political involvement of the church of the poor was not just confined to the actions of certain priests. The *Penitentes* dominated politics throughout northern New Mexico and areas of southern Colorado inhabited by Hispanics. The church authorities condemned such political involvement but could do little to stop it. At the edge of those same *Penitente* strongholds during the last part of the nineteenth century, a secret society called the Gorras Blancas waged war against the ranchers who had acquired large landholdings by questionable means. Their platform was "to protect the rights and interests of the people in general and especially those of the helpless classes." The church that Lamy created had no contact with, control over, or sympathy for these fighters for justice.

By the end of the nineteenth century, Hispanic Americans in the Southwest had no institutional voice in the church. The native Hispanic priests who had been their spokesmen in mid-century had all been purged or died out. The removal of the activists had been a powerful lesson for those aging priests who remained. They had realized that they could remain only on condition that they were submissive. They had faded away quietly.

The Hispanic laity, assumed to be inferior to the Anglo Americans and immigrants from Europe, simply returned to their old ways. For almost 300 years in New Mexico, 200 years in Texas, and 100 years in California, they relied, of necessity, on their own homespun religious traditions. These served them well.

Due to violence and lack of economic opportunity, Hispanic immigration to the Southwest was minimal during the latter part of the nineteenth century except perhaps in south Texas. At the same time, however, Hispanics were beginning to establish themselves in the Southeast. As Cubans struggled for their independence during the last half of the century, exiles began to settle in Tampa, Florida. After Cuba's independence following the Spanish-American War in 1898, the continued political turmoil stimulated ongoing migration to the United States.

On July 25, 1898, United States troops invaded Puerto Rico. The Treaty of Paris ending the war made the island a possession of the United States. During the nineteenth century, the population had increased from 150,000 to nearly one million.[34] The economic policies of the island's new rulers would create the conditions for a future mass migration to the mainland. Since Puerto Rico had been coveted to develop sugar production, North Americans soon acquired huge tracts of land for plantations.

The dispossessed peasants moved to the cities, increasing unemployment.

—4—

Growth and Conflict
(1890-1946)

Although in absolute numbers the Hispanic population increased in the last half of the nineteenth century, it had declined steadily as a proportion of the total population throughout the Southwest. This trend lent authority to the hypothesis that the Hispanic, like the Indian, was destined to disappear. The Church, accepting that view, acted accordingly. It gave first priority to the Anglo American and to the immigrants from Europe. The bishops and clergy did serve the Hispanic people but seemed to view such work as temporary. That is the inescapable conclusion of statements of the early French clergy in Texas expressing satisfaction at Mexican emigration.

About the turn of the century, however, a new awareness began to grow. It was as if, however dimly, the bishops and clergy realized that Hispanics were in the Southwest to stay and perhaps even to grow. Church leaders saw that the Spanish-speaking people were not only beginning to grow as a percentage of the total population but also spreading to other parts of the country. At that time, the bishops, pastors, and religious congregations began to confront the challenge seriously. Nevertheless, such ministry was, in many cases, supplemental to the main responsibility of serving the dominant society. Limits were placed on Hispanic ministry so as not to offend the Anglo. As late as 1940, Mexican religious practices that might be offensive to Anglo Americans were not permitted. Charles Buddy, the first bishop of San Diego, wrote that some practices were "a source of scandal and could easily weaken the faith of the people." He referred to dances held for the feast of Our Lady of Guadalupe and during processions of the Blessed Sacrament. Buddy canceled some of these demonstrations.[1]

TEXAS

In Texas Spanish-surnamed clergy began to appear. They were Spanish Oblates of Mary Immaculate and Spanish Claretians who established missions in the region during that period. Moreover, the religious orders and congregations of religious women which, in the past, had seen their primary mission as serving the new immigrants from Germany or France, now began to devote at least part of their ministry to Hispanics. This was particularly evident among the congregations of religious women. The Sisters of the Incarnate Word and Blessed Sacrament, for example, took over a hospital in Brownsville, which served mostly Mexican Americans. In Fort Worth, St. Paul Hospital started a free clinic in the Mexican section of town in the 1920s. In 1907, the Sisters of Mercy began opening schools throughout the Rio Grande Valley.

For the first time, Mexican Sisters started working in the Southwest. Shortly after the outbreak of the Mexican Revolution in 1910, the Society of Santa Teresa de Jesus took charge of a new parish school at Our Lady of Guadalupe parish and also at San Felipe parishes in San Antonio and in Uvalde. Driven north by the Mexican Revolution and by the religious persecution that followed, other nuns and priests came to serve the Mexicans in the United States. Five Sisters of Charity fleeing Mexico in 1927 opened a convent in El Paso. Soon joined by eighteen others, they founded a home for delinquent girls.

At the same time, spiritual ministry to Hispanics improved. Bishop Pedro Verdaguer, the apostolic vicar of Brownsville, increased the number of Spanish-speaking clergy even though he had a low opinion of the Mexican people. He said they were unindustrious and superstitious. Between 1911 and 1913, so-called "Mexican churches" were going up in many areas. In 1915, St. Joseph parish, headed by two priests with Spanish surnames, was founded in Fort Worth to serve the Spanish-speaking.

These were the beginnings of a separate church for Hispanics. In part, at least, this was a reaction to prejudice. Anglos were not willing to mix with the Mexicans even in church.[2]

In many places there was a church for Mexican Americans and one for Anglos. In other places, where the Hispanics lived in segregated neighborhoods, the Mexican churches were needed simply because there would be no other place for them to worship. By 1918, eighty-two new churches had been built in the Archdiocese of San Antonio alone, many of them for the Hispanic community.

Reinforcing the idea of separate churches, the clergy encouraged the Mexicans and Mexican Americans to form their own church organizations. In many parishes, therefore, *cofradias*, *sociedades* and *apostolados* were organized. Father Juan Maiztegui, C.M., founded the Association of Our Lady of Guadalupe in 1911 in San Antonio. This society, reorganized in 1932 as the Guadalupanas, spread throughout the Southwest and became the main guardian of the culture and religious traditions of the Hispanic people.

Around that time, Rome began erecting dioceses in areas with a proportionately high Hispanic population. In 1912, Corpus Christi was established, with Bishop Paul Nussbaum in charge. Though he had previously voiced prejudice against Hispanics, he doubled the number of parochial schools to eighteen before ill health forced him to resign seven years later. The next one was the Diocese of El Paso, founded in 1914. A. J. Schuler, a Jesuit, became the first bishop. He, like his contemporaries, built many schools, parishes, orphanages, and a hospital. Amarillo became the seat of another diocese in 1927, and R. A. Gerken the first bishop. A year later, San Antonio became an archdiocese.

During this period and for decades hence, the church of the Southwest, pleading that it was over-extended and lacking resources, dealt only with spiritual matters and devoted little effort to work for social justice. Even then, however, there were the beginnings of the social commitment of the latter half of the twentieth century. In 1930, Father Charles Taylor gathered 450 farm workers in Crystal City to discuss labor conditions and to demand labor agreements from the growers. Another priest called attention to the prejudice of Anglos, especially those from the northern part of the country, who saw Mexicans as a lower race and wanted nothing to do with them except to use them for manual labor.[3]

The bishops of Texas continued to depend on foreign clergy rather than develop local Hispanic vocations. But in 1942, a priest visiting St. Anthony Seminary called attention to six Mexican American seminarians studying there. He said they were the "future of the province."[4]

CALIFORNIA

California's Irish bishops also built many institutions, but they were largely for mainstream Catholics. An exception was Archbishop John L. Cantwell of Los Angeles who addressed some of the needs of Mexican Americans. He built clinics and, in the 1920s, spent more than half of the archdiocese's social welfare budget on them.[5] Father Patrick Browne of St. Boniface Parish in Anaheim set up four chapels to serve migrant workers during the same period. In Oakland, Father Charles Philipps of St. Mary's Parish served migrant workers. Other bishops and clergy, however, acted as if they were not aware that Hispanics were an ever larger part of their flock.

Archbishop Edward Hanna, who headed the Archdiocese of San Francisco from 1915 to 1935, was openly hostile. On one occasion he wrote to the California congressional delegation asking that immigration from Mexico be limited. The Mexicans, he said, "drain our charities; they and their children become a large portion of our jail population, affect the health of our community, create a problem in our labor camps, require special attention in our schools and are of low mentality, diminish the percentage of our white population and remain foreign."[6]

Content with the steady arrival of priests from Ireland, the bishops made less of an effort than in Texas to bring in Spanish-speaking priests or develop native vocations. Between 1848 and 1945, the Archdiocese of San Francisco had no Hispanic seminarians. Not one of its diocesan priests was trained in Mexico and, among those in religious orders, only one, a Jesuit, was from Spain.[7] In San Jose, which has always had a large Hispanic population, no Mexican or Mexican American served as a pastor between 1852 and 1962.[8] The Franciscans required their seminarians to take six years of German but apparently no Spanish.[9]

NEW MEXICO

When the fourth archbishop of New Mexico, Peter Bourgade, a Frenchman, was consecrated in 1899, two sermons were preached—one in English and one in Spanish. Significantly, the latter was by a French priest, not a native Hispanic. That vignette accurately characterized the Church in New Mexico at that time. The French and other foreign priests held the leadership posts. Hispanics were virtually if not totally absent from the clergy and religious congregations. On the other hand, they continued to be the overwhelming majority of the flock. In southern Arizona, where a similar situation prevailed, the bishops were French but the lay leaders were Mexican or Mexican American.[10] In Tucson, as in New Mexico, Mexicans were the majority of the population through the 1920s and 1930s. At that time there were six parishes in town, four for the Spanish-speaking and two for English-speakers.

As in other areas, there was great institutional growth during that period. Since the Hispanics were the majority, they were, at least in part, the beneficiaries of the schools, hospitals, orphanages, and other institutions constructed by various groups. Many congregations of religious women began their work at that time—the Sisters of St. Francis, the Dominicans from various foundations in Michigan, the Sisters of the Sorrowful Mother. After an absence of about seventy years, the Franciscans returned to serve in missions for the Navajo Indians. But in one area, that of native vocations, the Church continued its benign neglect.

In Fray Angelico Chavez's history of the archdiocese from 1846 to 1946, all the pastors he mentions have French or other non-Hispanic surnames. This situation continued until Franciscan Albert Daeger succeeded the fifth and last French bishop, John Baptist Pitaval, in 1919. That is the first time, in fact, in an account of many years, that an Hispanic priest is mentioned. Fray Chavez writes: "In 1920, Father Antonio Perez, eased out by the friars from the Cathedral rectory where he had been an assistant, founded the parish of San Jose in Raton."[11]

Daeger, however, moved slowly. He did not ordain anyone until 1929. "After many years of no native clerical vocations," Chavez writes, "Archbishop Daeger ordained three New Mexicans from 1929 on: Fathers Jose A. Garcia of Santa Fe, Juan T. Sanchez of Tome and Philip J. Cassidy of Mora."[12] Daeger established a minor seminary in Las Vegas but it did not last long. His successor, Bishop Gerken of the Amarillo Diocese, became archbishop after Daeger's death in 1932. In 1935 he started another seminary in Albuquerque and recruited Mexican Americans so that "they can go back to eat beans in the pueblo."[13] Gerken purchased buildings originally built for a Protestant school and reopened it as Lourdes School, a combination seminary and industrial trade school for boys. Nevertheless, only in the 1940s, a century after the visionary Padre Antonio José Martínez had shown that the region was ready to ordain its own clergy, was a determined effort made to recruit native Hispanic clergy in New Mexico. In the mid-1940s, Archbishop Edwin Vincent Byrne, who had been the first bishop of Ponce, Puerto Rico, founded Immaculate Heart of Mary Seminary in Santa Fe, which still exists as a college seminary.

During the 1930s and 1940s, only two native Hispanic priests receive any mention in Chavez's history. J. T. Sanchez built a large new church in Clayton. Jose A. Garcia, who had been ordained by Daeger, started a parish at Chaperito in 1935, then went on to serve as pastor to the historic church of St. Francis, which after 150 years as a mission had finally been canonically established as a parish. Under Archbishop Byrne he became pastor of St. Ignatius parish in Albuquerque and finally held the post of vicar general. "It was the first time that a native priest has held any position of note since Fr. Juan Felipe Ortiz was vicar general in 1846," Fray Chavez writes.[14]

REGIONAL AND NATIONAL STRUCTURES

For the first time during this period, the Church began to establish regional and national structures for the Spanish-speaking. In 1923, an immigration office was established by the U.S. bishops in El Paso. But the most significant developments came in the waning days of World War II. In 1944, Archbishop Robert E. Lucey of San Antonio sponsored a seminar for the Spanish-speaking. About fifty delegates from western and southwestern dioceses met for three days to discuss all aspects of the Church's work with Hispanics. A second seminar was held the same year at the request of Archbishop Urban J. Vehr of Denver. Delegates from California, Arizona, New Mexico, Colorado, Wyoming, Oklahoma, and Texas attended.

As a result, many dioceses in the Far West and Southwest established Catholic Councils for the Spanish-speaking that were later also organized in dioceses of the Midwest and Northwest where migrants worked in the fields. The following year, fourteen bishops organized the Bishops' Committee for the Spanish-speaking. With funds provided by the American Board of Catholic Missions, the committee's staff began an intensive program of social and spiritual aid in four provinces — Los Angeles, Santa Fe, Denver, and San Antonio. The first part of the program included construction of clinics, settlement houses, community and catechetical centers; the second, services for migrant workers, such as maternal and child care, improvement of recreational and educational opportunities. A regional office was established to direct the work.

The immediate goals of the committee were to improve housing, nutrition, infant and maternal health, and to reduce delinquency. The long-term goals were to make the Hispanic people better Catholics, to improve educational and economic opportunities, and to eliminate discrimination and prejudice. The problem existed not only in society at large but also within the Catholic Church. In California, Anglo Catholics withdrew their children from parochial schools when they were opened to Mexican children.[15]

In part, the bishops decided to begin special programs to defend against Protestant proselytism, which they saw as widespread. Almost every report by the committee mentioned the progress made in that area. In 1946, for example, it mentioned that *"Somos Catolicos"* (We are Catholics) posters had been printed and distributed to the Spanish-speaking. "Pastors will urge members of their flock to display these stickers on their front doors as means of discouraging Jehovah's Witnesses and other house-to-house proselytizers."[16]

But more importantly, the bishops formed their committee and established the councils and the regional office because they had changed. While in a previous time they had claimed that their proper sphere was the spiritual realm—to prepare the faithful for life after death—now they felt impelled to take a stronger role in seeking social justice. Perhaps it was because they had realized their inconsistency in this regard. In the case of the Irish, for example, the Church had fought hard to overcome prejudice and to help the workers organize into labor unions. The bishops and clergy did not beg off, as they did when facing the injustice suffered by Hispanics, that the business of the Church was not of this world.

Now, the bishops asked that better wages be paid to Mexican American farmworkers, that pit privies be eliminated in the barrios, that water, lights, and sewers be installed and streets be paved. The committee helped pastors to open employment bureaus, conduct naturalization classes, and organize Catholic War Veterans.

The leaders among the bishops were Archbishop Lucey, an early advocate for Mexican American rights, and Samuel Cardinal Stritch of Chicago, who was head of the American Board of Catholic Missions, the chief source of funds for the committee's programs. During a visit to Texas, he had been "horrified at the kind of life most Mexicans lived. Their condition seemed to him worse than that of Negroes of the old South." His offer to seek funds "to attack these fundamental ignominies" made the programs of the Bishops' Committee possible.[17]

THE GROWTH OF THE CHURCH OF THE POOR

The key event in the growth and spread of the Hispanic population in the United States during the first part of the twentieth century was the Mexican Revolution, which began in 1910. It was the bloodiest war in the Western Hemisphere, lasting ten years and causing far more casualties than the Anglo American civil war. It took more than a million lives and caused hundreds of thousands of refugees to leave the country. Moreover, it was followed by another ten years of turmoil, including religious persecution and the Cristero war between lay Catholics and the government from 1926 to 1929. Between 1910 and 1925, the United States admitted 660,000 Mexicans legally, while an estimated 300,000 came without permission.

In addition to immigrants who came to stay, in the 1880s Mexicans began coming for temporary work when the railroads, the mining companies, and agricultural enterprises began recruiting workers to replace the Chinese excluded by the Chinese Exclusion Act of 1882. World War I increased the need for such workers. As a result, the Bureau of Immigration changed its rules in 1918 to admit Mexicans for work in agriculture, the railroads, the mines, and in construction. A total of 72,862 workers entered between 1917 and 1921. During World War II, the State Department negotiated an agreement with the government of Mexico to permit the entry of Mexican "braceros," as such workers came to be called, to come to the United States for seasonal work in agriculture. Between 1942 when the arrangement was made and 1964 when it was finally canceled by Congress, 5.2 million Mexican workers participated in the program. During the peak year, 1956, a total of 445,197 braceros worked on farms from coast to coast.[18] These legal programs, in turn, stimulated illegal migration, for there were many more applicants in Mexico than were accepted. Entry was easy because until 1924 the border with Mexico was open. At that time, Congress established the Border Patrol with a $1 million appropriation authorizing the hiring of 450 employees.[19]

When jobs became scarce or the economy declined, the authorities deported large numbers of Mexicans. In the first big expulsion, between 1920 and 1921, vigilantes, encouraged by labor leaders and politicians, terrorized Mexicans, causing the repatriation of 100,000. During the Great Depression of the 1930s, hundreds of thousands, many of them legal residents or citizens, were sent to Mexico in order to save on welfare costs. As a result, the Mexican population in the United States declined from 630,000 to 377,000 in 1940.[20] The deportations originated in many cities on the West Coast and Midwest. In Detroit the Mexican consulate arranged for the departure of the

Mexicans. Between 1931 and 1934 the Los Angeles Department of Social Service hired fifteen special trains, each transporting about 1,000 persons to Mexico City. Many of those deported were citizens or legal immigrants. The Church remained silent, however, in the face of such injustice. *The Tidings*, diocesan newspaper of the Archdiocese of Los Angeles, carried only one small item on the repatriations.

During the first three decades of the twentieth century, Hispanics experienced more violence than ever before. It seemed "as though there were open season" along the border.[21] From 1908 to 1925, as many as 5,000 civilians — the exact number will never be known — died in lawlessness so widespread that a federal official warned the governor of Texas that action would have to be taken to protect the victims.

Often those responsible for the violence were the Texas Rangers, who had evolved from "ranging companies" organized in 1823 to repel Indian attack. Though the Rangers have been idolized as heroes of the West, an investigation in 1919 revealed that they had committed murder, intimidation, torture, flogging, and widespread disregard for the law.[22] One historian said the Rangers "waged persecution," including threatened castration and legalized murder. Though he said some of the violence may have been understandable because the Rangers dealt with some of the cruelest outlaws who ever lived, "enough of this reprisal fell on people innocent of any crime but that of being Mexican."[23]

Time magazine reported that during World War II "the Rangers became little more than terrorists, a racist army for the purpose of intimidating Mexicans on both sides of the border."[24] The Rangers often made raids into Mexico to bring back cattle and horses allegedly stolen from Texas ranchers. One time a troop looking for rustlers executed all the men of a Mexican village in the mistaken belief that they were the thieves. On other occasions they drove Mexican Americans away to make more land available for Anglo Americans. The Rangers had the "visceral belief that the Anglo had exclusive rights to the political, educational and economic processes."[25] There is no record that the bishops of the Southwest protested against the epidemic of violence during that period.

MEXICAN MIGRATION TO THE MIDWEST AND EAST

Until the beginning of the twentieth century, the Mexican American population of the United States had largely remained in the states acquired by conquest more than fifty years earlier — Texas, New Mexico, Arizona, California, and the fringes of states bordering them. But soon after, colonies began to spring up in many parts of the Midwest and even in the East. The Hispanic population of Kansas went from 71 Mexicans in 1900 to 8,429 in 1910 and 13,770 in 1920; Michigan increased from fewer than 100 in 1900 to more than 8,000 by the end of World War I; Illinois went from 156 in 1900 to 4,032 in 1920; and Nebraska from 27 in 1900 to 3,611 in 1920. Even New York registered an increase from 353 in 1900 to 2,999 in 1920. Few were the states that did not receive immigrants from Mexico between the beginning of the century and 1930. Between 1926 and 1927, money orders were sent to Mexico from forty-four of the forty-eight states.

Following the route used by traders and trappers to infiltrate New Mexico during the Mexican period, Mexicans now used the same Santa Fe trail going the other way. Many of them came to work on the railroads. As early as 1907, they began to work as track laborers in Illinois. By 1910, 21 percent of the maintenance forces of the Santa Fe, Rock Island, and Galesburg and Aurora divisions of the Burlington Railroad were Mexican. Those percentages increased to 75 percent of the Santa Fe workers in 1927 and 80 percent of Burlington's by 1928. Others worked in meat packing houses, steel mills, tanneries, and cement plants. In 1928, Mexicans were 12 percent of the workers in eight large plants of basic industries.

Heretofore, the migrants or immigrants who had come north to the United States had settled in the Southwest and worked in agriculture. They traveled to the Midwest and other areas as agricultural workers with some of them gradually leaving farm work to settle in small towns. But the Mexican immigrants who came during the first three decades of the twentieth century were recruited directly into industrial jobs in the big cities, according to agreements with the Mexican government. For example, in 1923 the Bethlehem Steel Company brought at its own expense 912 men, twenty-nine women, and seven children from Mexico's central plateau to work at its plants in Bethlehem, Pennsylvania, Lackawanna, Ohio, and other places. The company's agreement with the consul general guaranteed wages and other benefits, including quarters and transportation back home for those who worked at least a year.[26] Similarly, the president of a steel company in Chicago brought several groups of Mexican workers from Chihuahua because he owned land there and knew the people.[27]

The recruitment of Mexicans became necessary after Congress passed the quota law, limiting the number of persons from any nationality who could immigrate to the United States to three percent of those already in the country by 1910. The limitations, which did not apply to Canada, Cuba, Haiti, the Dominican Republic, Mexico, and Central and South America, sharply curtailed entries from Eastern Europe. That opened up many jobs in industry and agriculture to Mexicans and Mexican Americans.

Catholics and their pastors did not usually welcome the Mexicans in the Midwest and East. Priests said the Mexicans were superstitious and attached too much significance to small devotions. "We have shut out the European immigrant and have accepted the uncivilized Mexican in his place," a priest in Gary, Indiana, said. He charged that there were 560 communists in Gary and most of them were Mexicans and Russians. He also complained that the Mexicans could not be Americanized.[28] Despite the tensions, the Church competed with Protestants in providing aid to the Mexicans in time of need.

At the same time as Mexicans were arriving in the Midwest from Mexico, Puerto Ricans were beginning to move to large eastern cities and, in smaller numbers, to work in agriculture in the East. The first migration occurred in 1900 when many went to Hawaii to work in the pineapple plantations. Between 1900 and 1909, however, only 2,000 came to the mainland. They did not start to come in large numbers until 1917, when Congress made Puerto Ricans United States citizens, in time for many of them to serve in the Armed Forces during World War I. After the war, few of the veterans returned to the island; the majority settled in New York, where a small community already existed. The migration increased slowly through the first four decades of the twentieth century. Between 1920 and 1929, 42,000 came; between 1930 and 1940, 18,000. The true exodus would not begin until the period following World War II. New York, where more than a million would eventually settle, had only 70,000 Puerto Ricans in 1940.

The New York archdiocese reacted to the growing number of Puerto Ricans (and other Hispanics, including Mexicans) by opening national chapels: Our Lady of Guadalupe in 1902, Our Lady of Esperanza in 1912, La Milagrosa in 1926, and Holy Agony in 1930. Our Lady of Pilar, founded in 1859, served the Hispanics who lived in Brooklyn. These chapels were "half-way stations" to provide the sacraments to the Spanish-speaking people until they could learn enough English to assimilate into territorial parishes. Many Puerto Ricans had the feeling that because they spoke a foreign language, they were considered to be not fully Catholic.[29]

The new Hispanic residents of the Midwest and East were welcomed neither in society nor in the churches. They encountered discrimination in restaurants, bars, barbershops, and in employment. Farm workers, however, received the worst treatment. They were welcome only as long as there were crops to be planted, cultivated, or harvested. What happened in one Michigan county was typical of many areas. When the harvest was over, the sheriff rounded up any stragglers and told them to leave. "There is tacit agreement among all groups in the community that the migrants must be out of the area by October," said one report.[30]

In this period the Hispanic population was gradually migrating to the cities. Until the 1930s, the Hispanics in the Southwest were largely a rural people. After World War II, however, they were one of the most urbanized groups in the United States. Several factors influenced the transformation. One was drought, another the Depression and, most decisive, World War II.

The war gave many an opportunity to acquire new skills and improve their earning capacity. Their performance exposed the oft-repeated lie that Hispanics were incapable of anything but common labor. The next generation would have a better chance to receive a good education. But these gains were not without cost. A people previously used to monocultural isolation found themselves in an environment of cultural conflict and often violence.

In 1931 a presidential commission on law enforcement said that the police in East Chicago, where Mexican colonies were established in the first decade of the century, put Mexicans "into the calaboose" even if they had only a breath of liquor, or laughed too loud at a party. "The police are bad to Mexicans," the report stated. "They do not wait for an explanation but catch every Mexican they suspect and hit him over the head."[31] Gratuitous violence, often from the police but sometimes from citizens, was a common hazard of urban life for Hispanics in the Southwest as well as in other areas.

Sometimes there was mass violence, as in Los Angeles during World War II. In August 1942, police ostensibly combating youth gangs blockaded streets, stopped every car and every pedestrian and arrested 600 youths, of whom 175 were charged with suspicion of crimes ranging from assault to robbery to auto theft. Any object that could be used in an assault—for instance, tire irons or tools in the trunks of cars—was viewed as evidence of criminality.

The campaign against Mexicans, abetted by inflammatory news stories, finally resulted in a riot in June 1943. Thousands of soldiers, sailors, and Marines, supposedly retaliating for the beating of eleven sailors by a Mexican American gang, rampaged through the streets of Los Angeles for an entire week. They assaulted hundreds of Mexican American youths and some adults while police watched, only to move in later to club and arrest the victims. When there was no one to attack, the servicemen sacked businesses. The disturbances were called the "Zoot Suit riots" for the pleated, high-waisted pants and long coats worn by gang members who were the supposed targets. But the victims included children as young as twelve and even mothers trying to protect them.

In the investigations that followed, public officials tried to absolve themselves for doing nothing to prevent or stop the violence. The press tried to justify its prejudicial reporting. The investigators, however, found that the police set off the violence to help the cause of an officer named Dixon who was coming to trial for kicking a drunk to death in the central jail. "By staging a fake demonstration of the alleged necessity for harsh police methods, it was hoped the jury would acquit Dixon," a journalist-historian wrote.[32] In other cities across the country, there were less and less newsworthy incidents attributable to the same cause: the resistance of Anglo Americans to the Hispanic urban settlers.

THE STRUGGLE TO ORGANIZE

The opening of the twentieth century marked the beginning of the struggle of Hispanics to win their rights in society. Anglo Americans would soon see behavior that would challenge the myth of the Mexican Americans as a docile people. Half a century of violence and oppression had, indeed, made them a people who would endure in silence. It was a mechanism for survival. As the novelist Mary Gordon wrote in relation to the Irish, "Silence too is another form of protective coloration not unknown by the oppressed."[33] But the new behavior, militant and demanding, indicated in part that the Hispanics were changing, gaining courage and confidence. Injustice rankles and, sooner or later, an oppressed people is bound to rise. But another cause was the arrival of immigrants who had not been conquered. It was perhaps they who made the greater efforts to organize Hispanics, especially in the fields, orchards, and vineyards.

For eight years the Industrial Workers of the World, founded in 1905 and dubbed the Wobblies, tried to organize farmworkers in California. But their leaders were thrown in jail, sometimes unjustly convicted, and their efforts ended in failure. Mass arrests and deportations led to the same fate for the first Mexican union, the *Confederacion de Uniones Campesinos* in 1927, which had 3,000 members in twenty locals in California. The Cannery and Agricultural Workers Union, which went on strike in the 1930s, fell victim to vigilante groups, the police and the courts. In Vacaville, forty masked men took six strike leaders out of jail, flogged them and then clipped their heads with sheep shears and poured red enamel over them. In Pixley, bullets riddled a union building, killing a husband and wife. No one was punished for those crimes, even though some of the perpetrators were positively identified. Instead, eight union leaders served two years in prison.

The response to a strike by cantaloupe harvesters who walked off their jobs in California's Imperial Valley in 1928 was typical of many other encounters. The sheriff falsely accused the strikers of being communists and arrested four leaders for disturbing the peace. Then he closed the offices of the union, declared future strikes unlawful, told the Mexicans they should go back to Mexico if they were not satisfied in the United States, arrested a newspaper dealer critical of his tactics, and even prohibited Mexicans to gather for any reason. The courts set high bail for the strikers.

But it was not just those charged with law enforcement who opposed the organization of the farmworkers. When Congress passed the National Labor Relations Act in 1935, it excluded farmworkers from its benefits. Government agencies such as the Immigration and Naturalization Service sometimes relaxed controls at the border to let in undocumented workers to defeat strikes. No one really believed that the workers were communists; that was just a convenient pretext for putting them down. What was at issue here was the one-sided social contract with the Mexican and Mexican Americans. They had a place in society only as long as they accepted their marginal status. Society condoned the shoddy treatment of farmworkers with assertions that they were happy following the crops, that they were getting much better wages than they would have earned in Mexico— even if they were American citizens and had never lived there— and that they were being treated justly.

The struggle in the mines was as difficult as in the fields. Troops were called out when Hispanic copper miners tried to organize in Arizona in 1903. They were protesting the fact that Anglo Americans were paid more for the same kind of work. The mining company sealed up the mine and told the strikers to go home to Mexico. In 1917 when copper miners went on strike again, vigilantes hired by their employer forced 1,186 miners to board railroad box cars and shipped them to Columbus, New Mexico. When several thousand coal miners employed by the Gallup-American Company in New Mexico went on strike in the mid-1930s, the area was placed under martial law, even though there had been no violence. There followed a mass eviction of workers, a bloody riot, and mass arrests. Jesus Pallares, a miner from Chihuahua, then organized the *Liga Obrera de Habla Española*. With 8,000 members, it forced the authorities to abandon criminal charges. But Pallares was deported. Labor troubles due to unequal pay continued into the 1940s. The mines were sometimes closed so that new workers could be hired at lower wages when they reopened.

In San Antonio, thousands of pecan shellers were on strike in 1938. The issue was wages, only $2 a week in 1934 and only slightly better afterward than on the piece-work system. When the workers struck, police beat and jailed them. The police chief closed their soup kitchen. His tactics were so repressive that the governor of Texas criticized his conduct. Yet the archbishop of San Antonio, Arthur J. Drossaerts, refused to support the strike. Instead, he commended the police for acting against "Communist influences."[34]

Besides labor unions, many other civic mutual aid organizations came into being in the twentieth century. Mutual aid societies flourished by the dozens wherever Hispanics lived. In serving a variety of needs, such as insurance, burial services, aid in emergencies, and the like, they provided cultural continuity and ethnic identity for the Mexican Americans.[35] Some of the mutual aid societies also worked for civil rights. One of the best-known civil rights organizations was the *Primero Congreso Mexicanista*, organized in 1911 to fight discrimination and repression, particularly segregation in schools. Another was the *Congreso de Pueblos de Habla Española*, established in 1939. The most interesting note about this group, which fought against race and class discrimination, is that it had not only Mexican American representation from the Southwest but Puerto Rican from the New York area. A third civil rights organization was *La Liga Protectora*, formed in 1914 in Phoenix, Arizona to oppose state legislation that would have placed limits on the hiring of Mexican Americans. The most important civic organization that appeared during the first half of the twentieth century was the League of United Latin American Citizens, established in 1929. Its overall goal was to make Hispanics good American citizens by encouraging them to learn English and adopt the values of the United States. It soon found itself, however, in the midst of the struggle for civil rights. Its legal efforts led to the desegregation of public schools in Texas and California. It also attacked the exclusion of Mexican Americans from juries and founded schools for pre-school children that became the model for the Headstart program.

Some historians see this period as a second defeat (the first being after 1846) for the Spanish-speaking people.[36] Those writers see the Hispanics once again withdrawing into their barrios and colonias into cultural isolation. But, in reality, the Hispanics by the end of World War II had spread all over the nation. The old barrios of the Southwest could no longer hold them. They had broadened their horizons so much that they could no longer be happy in isolation. They had gained skills but more important, a new estimate of their possibilities. They would never go back to the farm.

PART III

The Church of the Poor Comes of Age

—5—

The Struggle for Rights

Except as people sitting passively in the pews, Hispanics had virtually no institutional representation in the Church in the late 1940s. There were few Hispanic priests because up to then little or no recruiting of Hispanic vocations had taken place. Spaniards were the largest group of Spanish-speaking priests, but their culture and that of the Hispanic people of the Southwest were not the same. The Spaniards were apt to judge the people they served as backward. After three centuries of virtual isolation, there was a cultural gap if not a chasm. Few priests had come from Latin America with the immigrants. After the revolution, Mexico was left with only 230 priests; it could ill afford to part with any of them. A similar situation prevailed in Puerto Rico, its big migration to the mainland already under way.

The Hispanic clergy, native or immigrant, were not in significant roles. The office of the Bishops' Committee for Hispanics was headed by Anglo priests until 1967, when Father Henry Casso of San Antonio was named executive secretary.[1] At that time, too, a highly regarded Mexican American priest, Patricio Flores, was the state chairman of the Bishops' Committee. Hispanics were absent from the chanceries and from the offices of the National Catholic Welfare Conference, the predecessor of the current United States Catholic Conference. There was one exception, however, and that was Father John García. Beginning in 1949, he was one of four priests who spent twelve years going up and down the valleys of California ministering to the farmworkers, until then sadly neglected by parishes and dioceses.

Similarly, Hispanic laity were absent from leadership posts in chanceries, hospitals, schools, or universities — or in any other institution. Even in parish life, Hispanics seldom held the top posts of organizations, if they were included at all. The only thing they directed in the parish in Brighton, Colorado, where the author grew up, was their bazaar, which was separate from a similar festival held by the Anglo American parishioners.

The number of native Hispanic clergy grew slowly during the 1950s and 1960s. One reason was that few Hispanics qualified for admission to the seminaries. Few Mexican Americans, for instance, graduated from high school. Those who did often went to inferior schools, with the result that the rare ones who applied to the seminary often could not pass the entrance tests. Or if they did, they soon found themselves in academic difficulties. What's more, seminaries were not friendly places for the Hispanics. David Gomez, a former Paulist priest, said he became withdrawn in the seminary as he was ignored by his Anglo classmates. Living on the periphery of the white world but not invited in, he concluded that the promise of acceptance and equality was "a total lie and a doublecross."[2] Father Paul Baca, a priest from Albuquerque, described how Denver's Archbishop Urban J. Vehr came to give a talk at St. Thomas Seminary, a regional institution run by the Vincentians in Denver. In the presence of two Hispanic deacons, the archbishop said: "The reason I don't have Mexican seminarians is that they just don't meet my standard."[3] Behind such views was the belief that Hispanics were of such weak faith that they could not be priests. Another reason, seldom articulated, was that the bishops also subscribed to the idea that Hispanics were an inferior people. They felt that priesthood, like the officer class in the Armed Forces, was for whites only.

THE CIVIL RIGHTS MOVEMENT

The postwar period in the United States was marked by increasing integration. In civil society, the Supreme Court ruled in 1954 in its landmark case, *Brown vs. Board of Education*, that segregated schools were unconstitutional. The battle has been portrayed as one of blacks versus whites, but it also affected

Hispanics. In less publicized cases, the League of United Latin American Citizens had won important state victories that had set the stage for *Brown vs. Board of Education.* In 1945 in *Mendez vs. Orange County (Calif.)*, a federal court in San Francisco banned segregation of children of Mexican or Latin descent "for reasons of race, color or national origin." Then in 1948, a court in Texas ruled for the first time that it was unlawful and unconstitutional to segregate Mexican children in the public schools of Texas.[4] Integration began to take place not only in the schools but in other public accommodations.

The Catholic Church followed the same trends, trying to bring its various ethnic groups together, but the process actually began much earlier. The Church had begun phasing out its national parishes in the 1920s. This move was influenced by nativist prejudice that had led to the enactment of laws limiting immigration to a percentage of those groups already in the United States. In 1916 there were 4,765 foreign language parishes, 47 percent of the total; by 1948, that kind of parish had decreased to 1,535.[5]

The leaders of the Catholic Church and their followers felt that they had to be 100 percent American. That conviction led Cardinal George Mundelein of Chicago to order in 1916 that foreign language textbooks be dropped from the Catholic schools. Such "Americanization" efforts were also directed at Hispanics. In 1918, the National Catholic War Council gave $50,000 to Bishop Cantwell of Los Angeles for Americanization work, which *The Tidings*, the diocesan newspaper, declared as "preeminently a Catholic responsibility."[6]

Americanization, however, proved to be a tragic mistake. Hispanic leadership, in the Church or in society, has come from two groups least affected by American culture, immigrants and long-time residents from areas such as New Mexico, south Texas and parts of California where Hispanic culture was not overwhelmed.

The 1960s also brought civil rights legislation that had an impact on the Church, specifically the Civil Rights Act and the Voting Rights Act, both enacted in 1964. These laws were a response to the highly publicized struggle for civil rights by blacks and, though less well known, also by Hispanics. Another national program that would force the Church to pay more attention to its Hispanic members was the war on poverty declared by President Lyndon Johnson in 1964.

In the Church, great changes were taking place as well. The bishops at Vatican II declared that the Church had to take a stronger role in the world. Since God had spoken in the history of all peoples, his word ought to be discovered and respected in different cultures. Suddenly, Americanization, previously an important element in the Church's ministry to Hispanics, no longer seemed wise. Among other reforms, Vatican II decreed that the liturgy should be celebrated in the vernacular instead of Latin. As far as Hispanics were concerned, that meant that Mass should be offered in Spanish and that their religious traditions should be respected, rather than discarded in favor of the religion of the melting pot.

At the same time, the Council documents demanding a stronger institutional commitment to social justice showed how far the Church had to move to fulfill its responsibility. This insight was enhanced by the documents of Medellín, the historic meeting of Latin American bishops in 1968, that elaborated on the message of Vatican II. In particular, the commitment of the Church to a special "option for the poor" contrasted starkly with the identification of the U.S. bishops with the economic interests of the middle and upper classes and the views of the political elite.

STRUGGLE WITHIN THE CHURCH

By the mid-1960s, there was a growing conflict between the *Movimiento*, as the Mexican American civil rights movement was known, and the Church. In general, Hispanics objected to efforts to deprive them of their language and culture. Some resorted to symbolic acts demonstrating that they and their religion were not being respected. In Mission, Texas, on the Sunday after Christmas in 1969, about one hundred Mexican Americans painted the statue of the Blessed Virgin brown.[7] In 1974, members of the militant Brown Berets took over the parish church in Brighton, Colo., and refused to let anyone enter until the pastor agreed to offer a Mass in Spanish each weekend.

Hispanic clergy and religious women and Brothers also

became aware that their training, whether by design or inadvertence, had caused them to reject their culture. Furthermore, they found themselves in situations where they could not serve their own people and where, in some cases, they were not permitted to do so. Father Patricio Flores, who was to become the first Mexican American bishop, said: "When I was ordained, I was sent to a parish where I was asked not to use Spanish to communicate with people who did not understand English."[8] A survey of Spanish-speaking Brothers showed that only eight percent were in full-time ministry to their own people and 21 percent in part-time work. The numbers among Hispanic Sisters were 25 of 961.

Hispanic priests, Sisters, and Brothers who asked to be assigned to Hispanic ministry encountered difficulties. John Cardinal Cody of Chicago rejected the request of Servite Father Alberto Gallegos and of another priest who asked to be reassigned to Hispanic ministry. That reaction was the common experience of many. Father Juan Romero of Los Angeles recalled: "In my first parish in Los Angeles I was not permitted to celebrate Mass or preach in Spanish in spite of the fact that 80 percent of the confessions I heard each week in the parish were in Spanish."[9] To many pastors, Romero indicated, it was more important to teach English than to proclaim the Gospel in a meaningful way. There was great anger among Hispanics when they realized that they had been unwitting accomplices in the neglect of their people by the institutional Church. As a consequence, some gave up their vocations and returned to the laity. Others opted to confront and demand that the Church fulfill its responsibility for Hispanics.

In time, many of the Hispanic clergy and religious men and women were able to gain assignments that permitted them to minister to their own people. That goal, however, could not be accomplished without organization. It also required a transformation of their own lives. Originally assigned to English-speaking parishes with the explanation that they had been ordained or professed to serve everyone, these Hispanic men and women gradually lost culture and, when they finally succeeded in being reassigned to Hispanic ministry, they were often no longer able to relate to their own people.

The Hispanics in the United States have been subjected to a process that communicated in countless ways the message that they and their culture were inferior. This has led, in extreme cases, to self-hatred; more often, to contempt for their own culture and people. The successful person tried to escape to the Anglo world, hoping to be accepted. Hispanics who entered the seminary or religious novitiate often wanted nothing to do with their own people when they were ordained or professed. What the *Movimiento* did for Hispanics was to reverse that process, to make them acknowledge their background and, better, to be proud of it.

"We are not ashamed of what we are," said Father Virgil Elizondo, a diocesan priest from Texas who became the leading Mexican American theologian. "We are proud of the heritage we have received from our parents and ancestors. We are proud to be descendants of our great Indian and European forefathers."[10]

Not all Hispanic clergy made the conversion, but those who became the leaders of the Hispanic church did. They became the true representatives of their people.

PADRES: CHAMPIONS OF JUSTICE

One of the organizations that came into being was PADRES, an acronym for Priests Associated for Religious, Educational, and Social Rights. On October 7–9, 1969, fifty Mexican American priests from seven states and the District of Columbia met in San Antonio. At the conclusion of their meeting, they called a press conference to announce that they had formed a new national organization to transmit "the cry of our people to the decision-makers of the Catholic Church in America."[11] The membership approved twenty-seven resolutions to present to the National Conference of Catholic Bishops at their annual meeting in Washington the following month. Father Ralph Ruiz was elected national chairman and Father Edmundo Rodríguez, S.J., was named national vice-regent.

PADRES made clear that it would be "the voice of the voiceless" Hispanics. In a letter of October 15, 1969 to Archbishop Francis J. Furey of San Antonio, Father Ruiz said: "We feel that we have a unique role as spokesmen within the Church for Mexican American and Spanish-speaking Catholics in the United States because most of us share the same language, culture, social *mores* and religious values of our people."

Among the resolutions were the following: that native Hispanic bishops be named in areas with heavy concentrations of Spanish-speaking people; that native Spanish-speaking priests be appointed immediately as pastors in large Spanish-speaking communities; that consideration be given to subsidizing low-income parishes from a national Catholic source; that high priority be given to inner-city projects involving priests more deeply in the day-to-day economic, social, and religious life of the people; that the church use its influence on behalf of the striking California grape pickers; and that seminary recruitment and education be expanded to include programs adapted to the needs of Mexican American seminarians and parishioners.

PADRES was especially harsh on the subject of vocations. Another letter to Archbishop Furey, dated October 9, 1969, said: "We *emphatically* reject as myth that the Mexican American has not given himself in sufficient numbers to the priestly ministry in the Church. All of us experienced during our seminary days the anxieties of many of our contemporaries who were forced out of the seminary one way or the other."[12] The letter went on to say that there had been systematic rejection, concluding: "We do not want to judge the motives of those who forced them out or kept them out, but we do know the fact that they were forced out or kept out."

THE STRUGGLE OF *LAS HERMANAS*

About a year later, Hispanic religious women began the process of organizing too. One of the catalysts was Victory Noll Sister Gregoria Ortega, who single-handedly tried to improve the lives of Hispanics in the Diocese of Abilene. Alone, with no title or support from the clergy, she faced down policemen, judges, school principals, and school boards, fighting for better education and working conditions. Some priests attacked her from the pulpit and eventually the bishop asked her to leave the diocese.

Ortega was joined by Sister Gloria Gallardo, who worked as

a community organizer and catechist in San Antonio's inner-city barrios. After years of working beside people struggling to maintain hope amidst chronic unemployment, health problems, and malnutrition, Gallardo decided not only to dedicate herself exclusively to her own people, but to help other religious women to make the same commitment. She said there were "innumerable cases" of Sisters who had asked their superiors to be allowed to work among their own people and had been denied permission.[13]

On April 2–4, 1971, fifty nuns from eight states gathered in Houston for the first meeting of *Las Hermanas*. Representing twenty religious congregations, the Sisters decided that the sole purpose of their new organization would be "more effective and active service of the Hispanic people by using the expertise, knowledge, and experience of religious women in the fields of education, health, pastoral work, and sociology."[14] The assembly declared:

> Sisters throughout the country have seen a tremendous gap between the relevancy of our consecration and our service to the People of God, especially the poor. We have searched for ways of closing this gap and have felt the urgency to become more attuned to the needs of the community so as to render better service to our apostolate. We, as Spanish-speaking Sisters, are greatly concerned with the plight of La Raza especially and are determined to better our efforts to meet their needs.[15]

One of the projects of *Las Hermanas* was to speak for hundreds of Mexican nuns who worked in seminaries, retreat houses, or colleges doing housekeeping, cooking, or other menial work. In one institution visited by *Las Hermanas*, each Sister was receiving only $50 a month. Such meager pay was going to Mexico to support impoverished congregations needing every cent to survive. *Las Hermanas* found that about half of these Mexican nuns would rather have been in catechetical work with Spanish-speaking people. Mexican nuns who came specifically to do such work often received little or no pay and were not even registered in the religious census because they were not citizens. "How can we as religious, priests, and bishops accuse the laymen of being unjust and exploiting our Mexican brothers when we are doing the same in the name of apostolic work?" asked Sisters Carmelita Espinoza and María de Jesús Ibarra of the *Hermanas* coordinating team. They further asked: "Is it necessary to profess vows to be a waitress or a house maid?" *Las Hermanas* began a program of educating Mexican nuns for the possibility of apostolic service, but the congregations in Mexico were nervous about losing the support, little as it was, from their members in domestic service in the United States.

THE MEXICAN AMERICAN CULTURAL CENTER

One of the effects of the organization of Hispanic clergy and religious was the founding of unique institutions to serve the Spanish-speaking people. One of the first was the Mexican American Cultural Center (MACC). It began in 1971 as a language institute because the promotion of the study of the Spanish language was the most critical need at the time. Six other institutes were added later. They dealt with culture, pastoral service, preparation of missionaries for Latin America, research and publications, leadership development, and media. Thousands of students came from all parts of the nation, Puerto Rico, Central and South America. Many of the faculty members were PADRES and *Hermanas* members who worked for a minimal salary so that the institution would succeed.

The creative spirit behind MACC was its president, Father Virgil Elizondo. In 1970, while teaching at the Incarnate Word Pastoral Institute in San Antonio, Elizondo became convinced that the Hispanic people of the United States needed an institute of their own. The idea won enthusiastic approval from PADRES when it was presented at their annual retreat in Santa Fe in February 1971. In September of the same year, the Texas Catholic Conference gave its unanimous approval to a motion by vocation directors asking for the creation of the institution. With Archbishop Furey heading the steering committee, the archdiocese provided buildings and housing on the campus of Assumption Seminary for an annual rent of $1 a year. Patricio Flores, who had become the first Hispanic bishop the previous year, was elected chairman of the board of directors. With his talent as a fundraiser, MACC was assured of survival. Eventually, MACC became the model for other pastoral centers for Hispanics. In 1988, such centers were in operation in Miami, New York, and South Bend, Indiana.

This period also saw the development of other church-sponsored institutions concerned with Hispanic affairs. In the late 1960s Father John McCarthy, director of the national office for Hispanics, which developed out of the Southwest Office for the Spanish-speaking in the 1950s, convinced Archbishop Robert Lucey, the most influential member of the Bishops' Committee for the Spanish-speaking, that there should be a regional office in the Midwest. For some years, Chicago had had a branch office of sorts, the Cardinal's Committee for the Spanish-speaking, organized in 1955. But an organization with broader scope was needed. The new office was established in Lansing, Michigan, in 1967. It served dioceses in Ohio, Indiana, Michigan, Wisconsin, Illinois, Iowa, and North Dakota. The person hired to head the new office was an Hispanic layman, Ruben Alfaro, a former migrant worker and barber, who traveled throughout the region encouraging dioceses to establish departments for Hispanics. He insisted that these offices should be headed by members of the laity, preferably Spanish-speaking. His suggestions were usually followed, with the result that many lay Hispanics became involved in the apostolate.

Hispanic offices were being organized in many other dioceses. As in the Midwest, many of them were headed by Hispanic lay persons. It was the only place on chancery staffs, almost always composed of Anglo Americans, that the Hispanic had a place. These offices, however, were a mixed blessing. While they promised that at least token efforts would be made to serve Hispanics, the result was that other chancery offices tended to do nothing, assuming that ministry to Hispanics was not their responsibility.

In 1967, the West Coast Regional Office for Hispanics was established by the bishops of California. Unlike the Midwest office, which has continued in some form since its founding, the West Coast office lasted only a few years. The main problem was that the two archdioceses, Los Angeles and San Francisco, refused to go along with the program.

Regional offices were eventually established (or re-established) in all parts of the country: Northeast, Southeast, Midwest, Southwest, mountain states, Northwest and West Coast.

The regional office established by the Bishops' committee in 1945 was given national scope in 1964 but did not come under Hispanic leadership until 1967. At that time Antonio Tinajero, a layman, was hired as director. In 1971, he was replaced by Pablo Sedillo, a New Mexican with a liking for politics. At that time, the office was moved to Washington and made a division of the USCC's Department of Social Development and World Peace. Sedillo's job was to lobby on behalf of Hispanics among the different departments of the USCC, but before long he was also lobbying on Capitol Hill. His efforts among the bishops won budget approval to hire four professional assistants. One traveled the country giving workshops on basic Christian communities while the others assumed responsibility for communications, for programs in the Northeast, and for programs on behalf of migrants.

A lack of direct communication with other divisions and departments, however, hampered the Division for the Spanish-speaking. Finally, in 1974, due to pressure from Sedillo and from PADRES, the bishops created the Secretariat for Hispanic Affairs, directly responsible to the National Conference of Catholic Bishops.

THE FIRST HISPANIC BISHOP

By that time, however, much more significant changes had taken place, thanks to the courage of Archbishop Francis J. Furey, of San Antonio. He did what no other bishop before had dared to do: he requested that a Mexican American be ordained a bishop. Shortly after being named archbishop of San Antonio in 1969, Furey requested that Father Patricio Flores, a man he had never met, be named his auxiliary. When the authorities asked for two more names, he returned the paperwork with Flores's name written three times. He explained: "If I had three Mexican Americans who were equally qualified, I would write them all down. To get an auxiliary bishop in Texas, we don't want to go to California. The auxiliary should be a native."[16]

Nevertheless, Furey had to sell his choice to the apostolic delegate, Archbishop Luigi Raimundi. "I told him we should have a Mexican American here because of the fact that we have so many [Hispanics] here. But the delegate said he had to make a report to Rome and they would ask him who started this and does he know what he is doing," Furey added. "So, of course, I had to do a lot of pushing because as you can imagine a break-through in the Catholic Church is not easy." Reminded that there had never been a Mexican American bishop, Furey said he replied: "That is an argument for me, not against me."[17]

That is how it came to pass that on May 5, 1970, Patricio Flores was ordained a bishop. (The date was doubly significant for all Mexican Americans: *Cinco de Mayo* is the anniversary of the day in 1862 when a ragtag Mexican army defeated invading French forces in Puebla, restoring self-respect after the debacle of the Mexican War.) The ordination, held at the San Antonio convention center because no church was large enough, drew 8,000 people. Cesar Chavez, the leader of the farmworkers in California, read one of the Scripture passages for the Mass. Thus it was that almost a century after the first black bishop was ordained in the United States (James Augustine Healy, ordained a bishop in 1875),[18] Mexican Americans had their first prelate.

Flores was a true representative of the poor. He was born in Ganado, Texas, the sixth of nine children of a migrant family. As a boy he and his family followed the crops north. Sometimes they lived in sheds. By the time he reached the tenth grade, attending classes only part-time because of the demands of migrant work, Flores had dropped out of school. He had felt the sting of discrimination, the gnawing of hunger, the despair of defeat. When he first expressed an interest in the priesthood, the priest in whom he confided turned him away. And when he finally won admission to the seminary, thanks to the intercession of a Sister and the goodwill of the bishop, he had to shine the shoes of his classmates to earn the money he needed for inci-dentals.

Between 1970 and the fall of 1988, twenty Hispanic bishops were ordained, almost half of them immigrants. Two were from Mexico, two from Cuba, two from Spain, one from Ecuador, two from Puerto Rico, and one from Venezuela. The others were native-born Hispanics. None, immigrant or native, showed the commitment to the poor that Flores did. For his first few years, before he became the ordinary of El Paso and then the archbishop of San Antonio, he was in a sense bishop to all Mexican Americans. Once again he followed the migrant trail to the Midwest and Northwest visiting squalid labor camps and bringing hope to the workers. When Cesar Chavez was jailed for defying unconstitutional court injunctions, Flores went to visit him. Once a grower who did not want him around barred his way with a shotgun aimed at his belly. But Flores was not intimidated.

Flores also spoke out on behalf of Hispanics in urban areas who suffered police violence or who were unjustly accused of crimes. Once he raffled off his episcopal ring for $2,200 to defend a 21-year-old man charged with a murder he did not commit.

Through his support, a powerful barrio federation—Communities Organized for Public Service (COPS)—came into being in San Antonio. It became a model for other such groups in Houston, El Paso, and Los Angeles.

Aware of how difficult it is for the poor to finance higher education, he established the National Hispanic Scholarship Fund in 1975. It has raised millions of dollars to help Hispanics get through college. Flores also was a strong advocate for the *indocumentados*, the illegal immigrants. He served for a number of years as chairman of the Texas Advisory Committee to the U. S. Commission on Civil Rights and he established the first diocesan office in the Southwest to deal with the problems of immigrants. Sometimes he personally tried to collect on the worthless paychecks issued by employers to undocumented workers. While visiting farmworkers in California a few months after he was named bishop, he arrived in Los Angeles at the height of the 1970 Vietnam War Moratorium march. Mexican Americans, protesting the high casualties and the disproportion of Mexican Americans among frontline troops, gathered in a park one Sunday afternoon in August to hear speeches. Police attacked the crowd after a minor disturbance and several persons were killed and many injured. Only Mexican American priests ministered to the dying and the wounded and the only bishop who would meet with the leaders was Flores, an act that earned him a stern reprimand from the cardinal archbishop of Los Angeles and the apostolic delegate. He had trespassed on another bishop's territory!

In addition to his commitment to social justice in civil society, Flores worked hard to improve the lot of Hispanics in the Church. On trips to Mexico he would keep an eye open to potential vocations. Once in Guadalajara, after he had become an archbishop, he noticed a young man standing outside the cathedral as he approached to celebrate Mass. The young man was still there when Flores emerged. So the archbishop walked up to him and asked: "When are you going to be ordained?" The young man, named David, said that once he had hoped to become a priest, but he had given up the dream because he felt that he had not lived a good life. The archbishop replied that he saw no impediment, and invited him to study in a seminary in the United States. Today David is a priest in San Antonio.

By 1987, with scholarship money from the fund he created, fifteen men from Mexico had been ordained for service in the United States. In addition, he had been able to save the vocations of Hispanics who had run into problems in the seminary. One of them was Father Jerry Barnes, in 1988 the rector of Assumption Seminary in San Antonio. He had been turned away by a religious order when he was only a year short of ordination. Barnes was never told why he was rejected; he guessed it was because he insisted on working with his own people.

Just as Flores encouraged Hispanics to organize in civil society, he strongly supported PADRES and *Las Hermanas* and other groups in the Church. He was the second national chairman of PADRES.

OTHER HISPANIC BISHOPS

Only one other bishop — Gilbert Chavez, auxiliary in the Diocese of San Diego — comes from a similar background. His father was a farmworker who picked grapes and oranges and harvested potatoes and other vegetables in San Bernardino, California. When Gilbert was fourteen years old, his father was killed in an accident. To support himself, Gilbert worked as a busboy in restaurants, as a packer in grocery stores, and as a laborer in the fields. He had to help support his family as well as pay his own way through Catholic high school. Like Flores, he had suffered deprivation and discrimination.

As a priest, one of his jobs for four years was that of chaplain at a state rehabilitation center for drug addicts. In a newspaper interview for his episcopal ordination on June 21, 1974, he said: "I have accepted the challenge to serve the poor, the Spanish-speaking, the Indians, blacks, and other minorities."

Unfortunately, he did not have the same support from his ordinary that Flores had from Furey. Then, too, his rhetoric was less polished, more abrasive. In a few years he had been effectively silenced, assigned to a border parish. He continued to work with Hispanics in the diocese but had no influence beyond the small circle of his diocesan activities. His short-lived efforts to be prophetic had foreclosed any opportunity he might have had to be an ordinary.

The same fate awaited Bishop Juan Arzube, an Ecuadorian ordained bishop in 1971 to serve as an auxiliary in the Archdiocese of Los Angeles. His being named had created disappointment among Mexican Americans, who wanted one of their own. Nevertheless, he set out to prove that he was a worthy shepherd. He championed the cause of a young lawyer who had been arrested in a protest against the Archdiocese on Christmas Eve in 1969. The State Bar Association had withheld accreditation for the lawyer, Ricardo Cruz, because he had been convicted of a misdemeanor as a result of the demonstration. The bishop spoke before the bar examiners and persuaded them to admit Cruz. He also made a courageous speech to the Catholic Press Association that stirred criticism from his brother bishops. In the late 1980s, he was still an auxiliary in the Archdiocese of Los Angeles.

One of the young priests Flores recommended for bishop was Ricardo Ramirez, who became his auxiliary and later the first bishop of a new diocese—Las Cruces, New Mexico. A Basilian who served as a missionary in Mexico and later as executive vice president of the Mexican American Cultural Center, Ramirez quickly won respect in the National Conference of Catholic

Bishops and became one of the most influential Hispanic bishops. He chaired the sessions of the Bishops Conference during the debate over the historic pastoral, "The Hispanic Presence: Challenge and Commitment." He also played a leading role in the writing and editing of the national pastoral plan for Hispanic ministry approved unanimously by the bishops in November 1987. Following in Flores's footsteps, he served as chairman of the Bishops' Committee for the Church in Latin America from 1985-1988 and was chosen over Cardinal Bernard Law of Boston as an alternate for the 1987 Synod on the Laity in Rome.

Ramirez also came from a background of poverty and would have to be classified as an activist. But because he has always tempered strong support for the poor, especially the immigrant, with a measure of prudence, he has avoided making enemies. Along with Archbishop Roberto Sanchez of Santa Fe, he is probably the most articulate of the Hispanic bishops. In the late 1980s, he was probably the bishop who was most active on a national level. Through his participation in CEHILA, he was well-known in intellectual circles throughout Latin America. He served as administrative secretary of the commission and wrote historical papers about the Hispanic Church in the United States.

If Flores is the model for the activists among Hispanic bishops, Archbishop Sanchez set the example for those who were called the pastoralists.[19] Whatever mark they have made has been more within the institutional Church than in civil society. Sanchez and Flores have contrasting backgrounds. Sanchez is a representative of the middle class, the son of an Hispanic lawyer and a mother of Spanish and Irish stock. Sanchez studied at the Gregorian University in Rome, where he was ordained in 1959. Later he studied canon law at the Catholic University of America in Washington, D.C.

At first it appeared he would be an activist in the mold of Flores. After his episcopal ordination, attended by 13,000 people, he took up a collection for the farmworkers and he asked pastors to urge support for the grape boycott then being waged by the United Farm Workers. Nevertheless, it soon became evident that he was less inclined to the affairs of the world than Flores. For the Third National Encuentro in 1985, he devoted his homily at the opening Mass to the Virgin of Guadalupe. Flores, on the other hand, gave a blunt talk on how far Hispanics had yet to travel to gain equity in the Church and in society.

Sometimes, however, he had no choice but to move out of the sphere he preferred. On February 2–3, 1980, there was a bloody prison riot in the New Mexico State Penitentiary that left thirty-three prisoners dead and ninety severely injured. Twelve of the twenty-five corrections officers on duty were taken hostage and subjected to such indignities that they were unable to return to duty. The prison facility was virtually destroyed.[20] The archbishop was summoned to Santa Fe to lend his assistance. At considerable risk, he went into the prison to remove the Blessed Sacrament from the chapel. But he did not play a decisive role in the negotiations that eventually ended the violence, for which some of the press was critical.

It was in the institutional church that Sanchez made his mark. He reconciled the *Penitentes*, alienated since the time of Archbishop Jean Lamy. He revived many of the traditions of the Hispanic people in the isolated villages of the diocese. He reversed the trend toward closing mission churches in small communities, and reformed the seminary to make it more responsive to Spanish and Indian cultures. On a national level, he headed the Ad Hoc Bishops' Committee for Hispanic Affairs for nine years, giving strong support to Pablo Sedillo in the Secretariat for Hispanic Affairs.

Many of the Hispanic bishops are more similar to Sanchez than to Flores. Loathe to foment confrontation, they are cautious on controversial issues of social justice. Along the border, it is a non-Hispanic, Bishop John Fitzpatrick of Brownsville, who has been the strongest advocate for refugees. Ironically, many Hispanics voiced disappointment when he was appointed in 1971. Activist Mexican American priests and nuns were particularly critical of the appointment. At great personal cost, Fitzpatrick has committed the resources of his poor diocese to defend the rights of refugees and immigrants. He supports Casa Oscar Romero, which has sheltered as many as five hundred refugees in defiance of federal policies he considers unjust. Furthermore, he adopted a simple lifestyle that is a model for other bishops.

Archbishop Roger Mahony, of Los Angeles, especially in his early years when he was the bishop of Stockton, has also demonstrated a commitment to the poor that Hispanics admire. A few others, among them Archbishop John R. Quinn of San Francisco and William S. Skylstad of Yakima, have also distinguished themselves.

One bishop who is very pastoral and who has responded admirably in time of crisis is Agustin Roman, auxiliary in the Archdiocese of Miami, and himself a Cuban refugee. When Cuban prisoners rioted and seized control of federal prisons in Oakdale and Atlanta in the late 1980s, they demanded that he mediate between them and federal officials who wanted to deport them to Cuba. Roman, despite frail health, went to the prisons and negotiated a peaceful settlement.

Some of the Hispanic bishops, however, are virtually invisible in the National Conference of Bishops. They made news when they were ordained and have not been heard from since. They do not often speak up at the bishops' meetings. Two are political reactionaries, supporting rightwing positions in Central America. As a group, they have failed, because of their differences, to create an effective lobby within the body of bishops. One said in 1988 that they could not even get together for a meeting.

By 1988, Hispanics did not seem as eager about having Hispanic bishops as they had been in the early 1970s. One of the leaders of PADRES, the Chicano priests' organization which lobbied so strongly for Hispanic bishops, said: "They [the Conference of Catholic Bishops] beat us at our own game." In the view of activist priests and nuns, the first four Hispanic bishops strongly supported their objectives, but those who came later were "meek and mild."[21] More often now the activist priests ask simply that whoever is selected be committed to the Hispanics. The assumption of PADRES and *Las Hermanas* had been that an Hispanic, by virtue of his ethnicity, would naturally take up the struggles of the people. It turned out to be an overly-optimistic estimate. In some cases it was a question of temperament. For others, there were barriers of ethnicity, class, ecclesiology, or political philosophy. The bishops from Spain, for example, bring a culture that harmonizes with that of a Puerto Rican only in superficial ways. One or two of the native-born Hispanic bishops had assimilated to North American culture to the point where they hardly spoke the language or understood the longings and aspirations of, say, Mexican Americans. Some of them were middle class and their values did not accord with those of farmworkers or of the urban poor.

As a group, Hispanic bishops show no greater commitment to Latin America than their Anglo colleagues. In February 1990 when the Conference of Major Superiors of Men asked bishops to sign a petition to Congress demanding that the Administration revise its policy toward El Salvador in view of the murder of six Jesuits by the military and other acts of persecution of the Church, the fifty bishops who signed it included only three Hispanics: Archbishop Flores, Bishop Arturo Tafoya of the Diocese of Pueblo and auxiliary Bishop Juan Arzube of Los Angeles.

Flores no doubt raised unrealistic expectations with his performance in the first few years. Few of his peers, however, were willing or able to accept the risks he took. In recent years, even Flores has been more circumspect. Age and illness have taken a toll. Asked about all this, he said that when he was first ordained bishop, he was all alone; now there are others who can speak out on the issues. But the younger bishops have not taken up his mantle.

THE ENCUENTRO MOVEMENT

In September 1971 Father Robert Stern, director of the Hispanic Apostolate for the New York Archdiocese, invited local leaders to meet with Father Edgard Beltran, formerly of the Latin American Episcopal Conference (CELAM) and then on the staff of the USCC's Division for the Spanish-speaking, to discuss a pastoral plan for Hispanic ministry. During the discussion Beltran said there ought to be a national encuentro (encounter) for Spanish-speaking leaders of the Church of the United States. The proposal received widespread support and finally the blessing of Bishop Joseph L. Bernardin, general secretary of the United States Catholic Conference.

The First National Encuentro was held in June 1972 at Trinity College in Washington, D.C. It drew several hundred participants from across the nation. The theme expressed by many at the meeting was that the Church had to change from a policy of assimilation to one of pluralism. John Cardinal Krol, president of the National Conference of Catholic Bishops, tried to head off such thinking. He said:

> While in God's providence there are people of many different racial, ethnic, and national origins in our Church in the United States, and while each group has something distinctive and very precious to offer to the life of the total community out of its respective heritage, in the final analysis there is among us neither Jew nor Greek, neither Irishman nor Pole, nor German, nor Italian, nor Anglo, nor Spanish-speaking, nor Black, nor white—but all of us one in Christ Jesus, all are descendants of Abraham.[22]

Respectfully, but sometimes in rather blunt language, the Hispanics replied that that was not true. There were Anglos, and they were discriminating against Hispanics in the seminaries. There were Irishmen, and, though only 17 percent of the Catholics in the nation, they were represented by 56 percent of all the bishops. There were Germans, and for a long time they had had bilingual and bicultural education in the Catholic schools. And there were bishops—but Hispanics were virtually excluded from their ranks.

As Bishop Flores put it: "From us have been stolen our lands, our language, our culture, our customs, our history and our way of religious expression. We have also been victims of oppression, discrimination, semi-slavery. We have been poorly paid for our work; we have lived in housing worse than that of monkeys in a zoo; we have not been admitted to some schools." In the face of all that, he charged, the Church had been silent. That was the tone of many of the presentations. It was a time to air grievances stored over many generations. At the end, the delegates drew a list of seventy-eight conclusions and demands they were making of the Church.

They demanded many things that eventually came to pass: that the Division for the Spanish-speaking become a special office or secretariat; that more regional offices for Hispanics be established; that there be a Bishops' Committee for Hispanics;

that more Hispanic bishops be named; that there be sections or special editions of diocesan newspapers in Spanish.

There were other demands, however, that would not be accepted: that basic Christian communities become a priority; that women be ordained as deacons; that non-territorial parishes be established for the Spanish-speaking; that mature married men be considered as possible candidates for the priesthood; that the training of all candidates for the priesthood in all the dioceses of the United States should include formation in spoken Spanish and Hispanic culture.

Archbishop Furey characterized the conclusions of the encuentro as the Magna Carta of Hispanic Catholics. But other bishops were less enthusiastic. Sedillo said: "We do not see the encuentros as a panacea. The whole idea is to create an awareness of where the Spanish-speaking are in relation to the local church and to show that the Church has in many instances neglected the needs of the Spanish-speaking."

The encuentro led to a repetition of the process at the regional and, in some cases, diocesan levels. It was seen as an opportunity for Hispanics to air their grievances. Sometimes these were fierce confrontations that were not understood by Anglo Catholics. Archbishop James V. Casey of Denver found it necessary to explain in the *Denver Catholic Register* that the archdiocese had not been pressured into holding the meeting:

> I want all of our people to understand that the questions raised at St. Thomas Seminary and the ensuing dialogue have happened because the Archdiocese of Denver issued the invitation for this to happen.
>
> The facilities of St. Thomas Seminary were gladly made available for the Encuentro for a two-day period. Bishop George Evans, Martin Work (a diocesan lay official), Father Hanifen and I went willingly to St. Thomas to listen and to learn, because the Church of Denver is concerned.
>
> We were not besieged by the Chicano people nor were we forced in any way to have these two days of dialogue, but rather the Chicano people were there because we invited them to express openly, their ideas, thoughts and frustrations.[23]

In other areas, the local or regional encuentros were less controversial, but they did give the Hispanics the opportunity to voice their opinion of how the Church ought to be responding to their needs. Though the National Conference of Catholic Bishops generally took a defensive posture when the conclusions were presented to them, they saw this as a useful process in dealing with the growing Hispanic minority. Five years later, they decided to hold another national encuentro.

The Second National Encuentro, held in Washington, D.C. in August 1977, represented a significant change. In the first one, the participants, as envisioned by Beltran, had been the leaders, mostly clergy and religious plus a handful of bishops. For the second one, thirty-four bishops attended, but the laity had a much larger role. First, there was a grassroots consultation of about 100,000. The committee preparing the Encuentro wanted to know from the people, members of Christian communities and never before surveyed about their views, what their needs were and how the Church could meet them. The results, organized at the diocesan and regional level, were brought to Washington by the delegates. While only 250 people had attended the First Encuentro, twelve hundred came to the second one: nearly five hundred as delegates and the rest as observers. Under the umbrella theme of evangelization, they discussed such topics as human rights, integral education, political responsibility and unity and the challenge of pluralism. In contrast to the first meeting, there were no talks, except one by Archbishop Robert Sanchez explaining the process. The rest of the time was spent in workshops.

Forty-five conclusions came from the Encuentro. Father Frank Ponce, assistant director of the Secretariat for Hispanics, synthesized them into five points. The delegates, he said, made a commitment to continue a process of reflection and growth in Christ as an Hispanic community. They resolved to form basic Christian communities, seeing that "it is here that future leaders are born and fostered." They resolved to correct injustices both inside and outside the Church, especially those suffered by migrant farmworkers and undocumented immigrants. "The delegates clearly gave notice that Hispano culture can no longer be ignored in teaching the Catholic faith," Ponce said. Finally, as a common thread in all the documents, they emphasized that lay ministers must be encouraged and recognized by the Church.

Unlike the First Encuentro, the second was conducted entirely in Spanish. This gave an advantage to Cubans and other recent immigrants who knew it well. At the same time, the Mexican Americans who were more accustomed to English became frustrated. For that reason, they had less influence on the final outcome.

The delegates asked the Church to be poor in spirit, to seek unity in diversity rather than in homogeneity, and to help eliminate economic disadvantage. They committed themselves to convert persons and structures in the Church so as to return to the simplicity of the gospel message. Nevertheless, the conclusions were neither so concrete nor so prophetic as those of the First Encuentro.

In 1983, the bishops approved a pastoral letter, "The Hispanic Presence: Challenge and Commitment," which called Hispanics a blessing from God and authorized the Third Encuentro. The process leading up to the encuentro began with a door-to-door survey of persons alienated from the Church. In Miami alone, the energetic Cuban-dominated apostolate visited 11,000 families. Afterward, most dioceses had their own encuentro, followed by regional meetings and, finally, the Third National Encuentro held at Catholic University in 1985. The process was facilitated by Brazilian Father José Marins, who helped Latin America's feuding bishops to achieve a consensus at their conference in Puebla, Mexico, in 1979. Now he played a similar role in unifying Hispanics in the United States around the broad outlines of a national pastoral plan for Hispanic ministry. The bishops finally approved the plan in 1987, but with no funds allocated to implement it, some Hispanic leaders compared it to a beautiful new car without wheels.

Not all Hispanic leaders are enthusiastic about the accomplishments of the encuentros. They suspect the bishops have embraced the movement because it provides high profile events that do not require a radical change in priorities. At a cost of $1 million every five to ten years, Hispanics can be pacified.[24] Nevertheless, there have been gains apart from whether the bishops have implemented the conclusions. In going through the process of the Third Encuentro, for example, many local leaders received invaluable training. Also, not waiting for a national plan to come forth, some dioceses put their own plans into effect. Moreover, the Encuentros have made bishops more aware of the need to serve and respond to the Hispanic community.

RENEWAL

Long before the encuentros, the *Cursillo* (Spanish for small course) had brought renewal to many American Catholics, both Anglo and Hispanic. An intense weekend experience of spiritual renewal, the *Cursillo* originated in Spain in 1947. Ten years later, two Spanish pilots training at an air force base in Texas introduced it to Father Gabriel Fernandez, of Waco. Soon Fernandez was conducting his own *Cursillo*.

Gaining quick acceptance, *Cursillo* was soon offered all over the country. It was given in both English and Spanish, with a directorate for each version in Dallas, Texas. By 1976, about 300,000 persons had made a *Cursillo*, including fifty to sixty bishops and about seven thousand priests and nuns. Unlike other movements, which fade after a time, it has continued to draw participants up to the present.

The *Cursillo* is a three-day program, experienced only once, of renewal and spiritual discipline. It combines charismatic and group dynamics techniques with an emphasis on sacrifice, confession, and physical acts of penance. Many of the Hispanic leaders of the 1970s owed their social conscience to the *Cursillo*, including Cesar Chavez and many of the farmworkers in his union.

The *Cursillo* also played an important role in the life of Patricio Flores. As an assistant at Holy Name Parish in Houston, where he spent his first seven years as a priest, Flores was forbidden to speak Spanish to Mexican American parishioners, even when they addressed him in that language. The pastor, Father John J. Cassata, later the bishop of Fort Worth, held that loyalty to the United States required that one speak English at all times, even in church. The *Cursillo* provided a needed outlet for Flores, if only for the opportunity to speak in Spanish. Traveling throughout Texas giving *Cursillo*s, he gained the respect of many pastors who went on to recommend him to Archbishop Furey when he asked for nominations for bishop.

The movement was not initially accepted everywhere. While Flores was making his *Cursillo* in 1962, his own bishop, Wendelin J. Nold, was in Rome at the Vatican Council. Upon returning he banned the *Cursillo* in his diocese because he wanted nothing in Spanish even though the Council had replaced Latin with the vernacular for church services.[25] About a year later, however, Nold reversed himself, seeing how effectively the *Cursillo* renewed the faith of Hispanics. He put Flores in charge.

Even in more recent times, some bishops have looked with disfavor on the *Cursillo* in Spanish. For a time in the late 1970s, Archbishop James V. Casey of Denver banned the *Cursillo* in Spanish, not, he claimed, because he objected to the language but because he thought that having it only in English would help bring Anglos and Hispanics together.

In 1976 only thirty-nine dioceses had a secretariat for *Cursillos* in Spanish. The directors, unhappy because they felt that many of their ideas, initiatives, and apostolic concerns clashed with those of the English secretariats, voted to establish their own national office. Only the concerted efforts of Bishop James Rausch, general secretary of the National Conference of Catholic Bishops, headed off the split.

Louis J. Reicher, ordinary of the Diocese of Austin, was the first bishop to give the *Cursillo* his approval, in 1959. By the middle of the 1970s, the *Cursillo* was active in 120 of the 156 dioceses in the nation. In New York, seventeen persons made it in 1958. By 1976, 14,000 Hispanics had taken part in *Cursillos* in Spanish. Quick to recognize its value, Francis Cardinal Spellman provided a meeting place. *Cursillos* in Spanish have been held continuously, but the English version was discontinued for a time. By 1976, 164 *Cursillos* had been given for men and 125 for women, all in Spanish. The reception in Brooklyn was just as impressive.

Another movement imported from Spain was Marriage Encounter. This movement, founded by Father Gabriel Calvo, was brought to the United States in 1968 by sixty couples sponsored by the Christian Family Movement. When they arrived in Los Angeles, the chancery, suspicious of what the new movement would bring, did not want to provide them with an official forum. The sponsors finally found a place to meet in Soledad Parish in East Los Angeles. About the same time Maryknoll Father Donald Hessler and a Mexican couple, Alfonso and Mercedes Gomez, led a Marriage Encounter at Notre Dame University. By 1973, more than 17,000 couples had experienced the weekend sessions intended to revitalize marriages. Three years later, the movement had grown to 77,000 couples. An estimated sixty thousand people from Marriage Encounter groups throughout the nation gathered in Veterans Stadium in Philadelphia on August 2, 1976, for an evening liturgy during the Eucharistic Congress.[26]

Another movement, *Movimiento Familiar Cristiano* (MFC) is similar to the Christian Family Movement (CFM), but unlike the latter, which seems to have faded on a national level, it is still going. Originating in the 1960s like the CFM, the MFC has representation all over the country and is conducted in Spanish. About three thousand couples belonged to it in 1988. MFC seeks to develop stronger families and better communities where people can live in harmony. It focuses first on marriage, then on the family and the community.

BASIC CHRISTIAN COMMUNITIES

Organizing basic Christian communities (BCCs) was from the beginning a top priority of the Secretariat for Hispanics. After the chief promoter, Father Edgard Beltran, became a layman and left his post, the impetus to organize BCCs came from parish and diocesan personnel.

In the Diocese of San Bernardino, Sister Rosa Marta Zarate began organizing BCCs among Hispanics in the 1970s, but her work was opposed by some pastors and, as a result, Zarate was no longer working in the diocese in 1988. Similar problems occurred elsewhere. Griselda Velazco, a member of an interfaith community in Chicago, said her pastor told her, "I wish you much luck even though you will fail." Nevertheless, the group was so successful that it became a model for others. In the Santa Fe archdiocese, a leadership development team trained leaders for the BCCs; in San Diego, Bishop Chavez started an evangelization team that trained animators for the small communities.

Though the laity has been enthused, the BCCs have often lacked the episcopal support they enjoy in Latin America. The bishops as a group have been ambivalent. When communities were proposed by the First Encuentro, the committee of bishops that examined the conclusions did not embrace the idea. But in their 1983 pastoral on Hispanics, the bishops called on the communities, along with other groups, to be a prophetic voice. The 1987 pastoral plan approved unanimously by the bishops makes the communities a priority.

In recent years, many local Hispanic apostolic ministries and movements have begun. In Miami, for example, the Cuban laity have instituted a dozen movements in Spanish, including the *Cursillo* and Family Encounter Movement, *Camino al Matrimonio*, a marriage preparation movement, the Youth Encounter Movement, the confraternities of Our Lady of Charity, the Legion of Mary in Spanish, the Catholic University Group, and the Charismatic Movement in Spanish.

These initiatives have not always been welcomed. In the late 1970s, Cubans felt that at least some Church leaders did not see their apostolic movements as instruments of service. Monsignor Bryan O. Walsh, former episcopal vicar for the Spanish-speaking said: "Many of the difficulties but not all can be traced to what I would call a reluctant acceptance by the Church of cultural and language differences as a necessary evil during a limited period of adaptation."[27] In Miami and elsewhere the issue was whether and to what extent Hispanics would put their own stamp on the Church.

—6—

Ministers and Ministry

The Hispanic population has grown rapidly since World War II. In 1950, there were four million Hispanics in the United States; in 1960, 6.9 million; in 1970, 10.5 million and in 1980, 14.6 million. Between then and 1987, they increased by 4.3 million or 30 percent.[1] At that time there were 18.9 million, broken down into 11.7 million Mexicans, 2.2 million Puerto Ricans, one million Cubans, 1.1 million Central and South Americans, and 1.5 million "other Hispanics" who do not fit in any of the other categories. By the year 2,000, according to one projection, Hispanics will total 25 million, rising to 30 million by 2010.[2] At that time, they will be the majority of Catholics in the nation. Yet, given current trends, they will be no more visible than they are today. They will not have a tenth of the nation's 400 bishops or of the 53,000 priests. Furthermore, they may be no more numerous in the pews. A New York study found that only 30 percent of Hispanic Catholics attend Mass four times or more a month, compared with about 50 percent for Anglos. The attendance may be even lower in the future. According to documents of the Third National Encuentro, only five percent of Hispanic youth attended Mass regularly.[3]

The traditionally low Mass attendance of Hispanics is at least partly due to the legacy of neglect and discrimination. In the Southwest, where parishes were few and far apart, the people became accustomed to have Mass in their chapels only rarely. They did not have the habit of frequent attendance because the liturgy was simply not available. In other cases, Anglo hostility made attending Mass an unpleasant experience. Furthermore, in Hispanic religiosity, failure to attend Mass regularly was not considered as grievous a sin as in Anglo belief.

Low participation has sometimes been used against Hispanics. In 1978, when Father Phillip Straling instead of Bishop Gilbert Chavez was named the ordinary of the new Diocese of San Bernardino, Hispanic activists protested that the choice should have been Chavez, on the grounds that Mexican Americans represented 65 percent of the local Catholic population. In response, however, it was argued that only 15 percent of the Hispanics were "practicing" and thus it was unfair to call them the majority.

There is no question, however, that Hispanics are disproportionately under-represented among the clergy and religious. Proportional to their numbers in the 1980s, there should have been at least 17,000 priests. Instead there were only 1,400. The same disparities applied to Sisters and Brothers. What was worse, only about 180 of the Hispanic priests were native born, the rest having been born in Spain or Latin America. In the last half of the 1980s, someone visiting the seminaries was likely to get the impression that Hispanic enrollment was growing rapidly. But Father Gary Riebe, S.V.D., who headed an Hispanic vocation project for the Bishops' Committee on Vocations, said that the impression was erroneous. Hispanics were proportionally more of the seminarians only because the number of Anglos had declined.

One reason there are few Hispanics in the priesthood or religious life is that there is no tradition for such choices. And there is no tradition because Hispanics were not recruited for the priesthood until after mid-century and, even then, not by all bishops.

Poverty has denied many the education they need to qualify for admission and to persevere in their studies. Until recently, few Hispanics graduated from high school and fewer still (less than five percent) from college. Even in the 1980s, almost half of all Hispanics dropped out of school before completing the 12th grade. Poverty, too, is to blame for a reluctance of parents to encourage their children to choose religious vocations. Sons and daughters must contribute toward the support of the family.

In recent years, religious orders and some dioceses have started special houses of formation for Hispanics. Riebe, a member of the Society of the Divine Word, was the pioneer. His house of formation, in the barrios of East Los Angeles, became the model for others. In 1989, there were fourteen such houses in Los Angeles alone. They provided remedial education when needed, training in skills necessary for success in college and the cultural reinforcement Hispanics often fail to find in the seminary.

It has been much easier to involve the laity in ministry. When Bishop John Fitzpatrick of Brownsville invited applications for lay ministers in the diocese, 450 Hispanics applied. That willingness is evident in young and old alike. In New Mexico, hundreds between the ages of ten and seventy make a hundred-mile pilgrimage for vocations annually; hundreds more assist the pilgrims along the way. That spirit expresses itself in different ways in many areas. Hispanic deacons, usually not reimbursed for their expenses, devote many hours to their ministries.

One permanent deacon, Antonio Sandoval, gave up a tenured faculty position as a chemistry professor at the University of Missouri in Kansas City to devote himself full-time to Hispanic ministry in Colorado. Told that deacons in the Archdiocese of Denver received no pay, he established a missionary society to support him and others whom he recruited. Somehow, he survived financially, spending his life savings to do his pastoral work and educate his three children. And the range of his activity was amazing. He was like an old-time circuit rider, going from Denver to Burlington on the Kansas border, 180 miles away. He preached in half a dozen or more parishes, founded Bible-study and prayer groups, went door-to-door to bring back people who had left the faith, gave several talks on radio each week on the Scripture of the Sunday Mass, and worked with migrant farmworkers who had no one to serve them. But when Archbishop J. Francis Stafford became the ordinary of Denver he asked Sandoval to dissolve the mission society. Fortunately, the deacon was able to get work in a parish. He reincorporated as a nonprofit educational society so as to be able to provide educational aid for migrants. In 1989, when a new pastor was named, Sandoval's contract was not renewed. Discouraged, he was forced to give up full-time ministry.

Hispanics in the 1980s were still vastly under-represented in the Catholic press. Only one headed a publication with national scope, a Catholic magazine. Few were editors of diocesan newspapers or Catholic journals. The only publications they headed, and not always, were Spanish-language editions or sections of diocesan newspapers. They were similarly absent from the faculties of Catholic universities and seminaries, leaving Hispanic students or seminarians without models to follow or advisers who had shared the same experience. Church boards and commissions had only token Hispanic representation.

Hispanics were not prominent in national peace and refugee movements. Fighting battles closer to home, in the barrios where they lived and worked, they lacked the energy for other issues.

One of the big frustrations of Hispanic leaders was the lack of funding for Hispanic institutions. The Mexican American Cultural Center (MACC) and others like it, plus the regional offices for Hispanics, found themselves constantly having to beg for funds. Dioceses funded them reluctantly. MACC had to depend on the transient largesse of foundations and religious orders. Though it raised about half of its annual budget, it had not developed sponsorship among Hispanics.

"I just hope that to continue having MACC all of us who have benefited from it will contribute, especially in a financial way," said Bishop Ricardo Ramirez, who served as vice president of the Center for several years. "We cannot be beggars all our lives, on the receiving end all the time. We must not only own it because we feel good about MACC. We must dish out."

The bishops have consistently refused to develop special funding for Hispanic institutions on a more rational basis. While allowing a national collection for black Catholics, they have refused to do the same for Hispanics. The American Board of Catholic Missions has been generous toward pastoral centers like MACC, but sometimes drastic cuts have created a crisis.

THE CHURCH'S SPECIAL SERVICE TO HISPANICS

The establishment of the Bishops' Committee for the Spanish-Speaking in 1945 reflected an acknowledgment that Hispanics had special needs not being met through the Church's traditional apostolates. In a sense, it was recognized that there were two churches. The programs started by the committee, while meeting some spiritual and social needs, also served other interests. One was Americanization, through which the Church enhanced its status in society. Another objective was to frustrate Protestant proselytizing.

But at no time was that special service to Hispanics more than a secondary mission. The bishops were at all times conscious that the Church's lifeblood, in terms of vocations, status, and source of funds, came from the Anglo community. Therefore, they were careful never to jeopardize that support. For that reason they were slow to oppose the Bracero program. Naively, the bishops thought they could achieve their goal of bettering the lives of farmworkers without antagonizing growers. At one point Father James L. Vizzard, S.J., head of the Catholic Rural Life Conference, declared:

> Church authorities often are frozen with fear that if they take a stand with the workers the growers will punish them in the pocketbook. .... Church institutions do not exist for their own sake. Nor does the Church itself exist solely for the comfortable, affluent, and powerful who support those institutions. Christ had a word to say about the shepherd who, out of fear and because the sheep weren't his, abandoned the sheep when they were under attack.

In 1950, the Bishops' Committee staff sought to improve low farm wages by consulting Catholic landowners in the Rio Grande Valley who, according to the staff, were "ready and willing to work out a just wage system." The committee thought the example and influence of Catholic growers would influence those who sought "to keep the laboring masses in wage slavery."[4] In the Diocese of Green Bay, the priest running the program for farm-workers, while recognizing the need to speak out unequivocally for social justice whenever conscience required, urged moderation to keep the goodwill of the growers.[5] The allocation of funds revealed how peripheral Hispanics were. The American Board of Catholic Missions gave $1.3 million to the Church in

Texas from 1925 to 1951. Of that amount $980,000 was spent in Anglo parishes and only $390,000 in Hispanic parishes. It was a state where even then two out of every three Catholics were Hispanics.[6]

While the service carried out under the auspices of the Bishops' Committee was an important step in light of the magnitude of the needs, it remained at best a gesture. In Arkansas, a 1956 survey revealed, there was only one Spanish-speaking priest to minister to 30,000 braceros. The previous year there had been none.[7] In 1953, the Bishops' Committee brought twenty-four Mexican priests to work in dioceses with the most braceros. They worked as far north as Michigan and Idaho, and the dioceses participating expressed satisfaction with the arrangement. But the program did not endure.

The Catholic councils for the Spanish-speaking, created by the Bishops' Committee in 1945, fulfilled an advisory role. While the Committee functioned in four episcopal provinces, the councils soon spread beyond. States with Hispanic agricultural workers soon had their own councils. As time went on, the councils were organized in Missouri, the upper Pacific Coast, Montana, and the upper Midwest. By the 1960s, with Puerto Rican farmworkers in states along the Eastern seaboard, there were councils in that region.

The councils were made up of a representative of the local bishop and other priests and lay people, including members of Catholic Action, the Confraternity of Christian Doctrine, women religious, school officials, the director of Catholic Charities, members of doctors' and lawyers' guilds, and so forth.

The councils fulfilled an important educational and social function. Perhaps for the first time in the experience of many of their members, Anglo and Hispanic Catholics sat down together to address common problems. Isolation has long been a problem between the two communities. The councils, trying to address that problem, included Spanish-speaking members whenever possible.

The councils strongly opposed the inflow of illegal immigrants. Father Raymond McGowan of the National Catholic Welfare Conference said: "The Catholic Council fights this invasion. It fights also for laws and unions to protect domestic farm labor on the commercial farms. It fights for laws, federal and state, to protect unions, wages, hours, and security in non-factory jobs . . . jobs which escape . . . the protection of nearly all labor law."[8]

Such eloquent rhetoric was rarely matched by effective action, but the councils did provide a forum to begin building an awareness of the problems. They sponsored annual conferences that drew an increasing number of participants and focused attention on pressing social issues. At the conference in 1962, there were representatives from twenty-six states, as well as Mexico, Puerto Rico, and Cuba. A reorganization leading to the creation of the National Office for the Spanish-speaking deprived the councils of a national role, but many continued to meet on a diocesan basis.

EFFORTS TO INTEGRATE TWO CHURCHES

Hispanics who moved into the cities after World War II had a particularly difficult time in practicing their faith. By then, Church policy had changed on national parishes. Other ethnic groups who had arrived previously had enjoyed a long period of adjustment during which strong community ties had been cemented through the parish. The Puerto Ricans, however, had no such opportunity. They were immediately forced to go to parishes where they were not wanted. While church leaders may have looked upon the process as integration, the reality was different. The Hispanics were kept apart in various ways. Encarnacion Armas, a long-time leader and spokesperson for Puerto Ricans, said her people had to attend Mass in the basement and they had to file through the alley to get there.[9]

In Brighton, Colorado, where the author lived, Hispanics were welcome only at the nine o'clock Mass every Sunday. If they went to any other Mass, they received hostile looks and sometimes were told outright to stay away. In towns in the Southwest that had one church for Anglos and another for Hispanics, life continued as usual. The integration did not occur until much later. At the First Encuentro in Washington in 1972, then-Bishop Patricio Flores said that although the signs "No Mexicans allowed" had been removed, the attitudes of rejection remained. In some places where migrant workers were occasionally allowed to use the parish hall, the building was fumigated immediately afterward.

Hispanics were not served well because the clergy did not know their language or have respect for their culture. Some dioceses began to recognize the problem. In New York, the Institute of Cultural Communication, founded in 1957, sent priests to Puerto Rico, the Dominican Republic and Colombia to study language and culture. By the end of the 1970s, about 600 priests and 200 nuns knew at least some Spanish.[10] Unfortunately, many other dioceses did not have a similar program.

Integration of the Catholic schools was more difficult. In some areas, Anglos withdrew their children when this was attempted. But in others, it did not occur because Hispanics lived in segregated neighborhoods. Nationally, only five percent of the enrollment was Hispanic in the 1970s. In some cities, like Chicago, Los Angeles, and New York, the breakdown was better. In 1979 in the Archdiocese of New York, 22 percent of the elementary students and 20 percent of those in high school were Hispanic.[11] In Brooklyn and Newark, the percentages were 15.3 and 13.5, respectively. But, at the same time, Hispanics were more than half the Catholics in the New York archdiocese and forty percent of those in Brooklyn. Hispanics therefore were still under-represented.

In other areas, however, not even this level of integration had taken place. In Philadelphia, where 100,000 Puerto Ricans lived, only half of one percent of the Catholic school students were Hispanic. In Washington, D.C., another city with a large Hispanic community, only 3.6 percent of Hispanic children were in Catholic schools. Generally, policy of the bishops aside, pastors did not expend great energy in creating one community out of their flock. In Colorado in the 1960s, pastors sometimes refused to witness marriages between Anglos and Hispanics. Even after Vatican II, some continued to refuse to offer Mass in Spanish. In New Mexico in the mid-1970s, a pastor in an Albuquerque suburb refused to allow a Mass in Spanish in a parish where 98 percent of the members were Hispanics. But he faithfully offered a Mass in Polish.

THE *MOVIMIENTO*

The Hispanic movement for civil rights, also called the Chicano Movement because of the name the activists chose to identify themselves, challenged the church to respect culture and religious traditions and work for social justice. Unlike the black movement for civil rights, which was led by ministers, the Hispanic counterpart was led largely by laypersons.

Hispanics were appalled at the hypocrisy they saw in their Church. On the one hand, they heard bishops and clergy asking them to adopt the trappings of American life. But when it came to demanding the right that gave meaning to being an American, they found themselves counseled in patience and acceptance of an unjust status quo. For this reason, the Church itself became one target of the *Movimiento*.

Hispanics demanded that the Church accept their language and culture. They further asked the Church to involve itself in the struggle of the poor for a more human life. It galled farmworkers that only non-Catholics, members of the Migrant Ministry of the National Council of Churches and Jewish leaders, walked alongside them on the picket lines in the vineyards of California. They were even more upset at the silence of the Church on key issues. "The migrant workers continue to live in the worst conditions in this country, and the church remains silent," Bishop Flores said in 1972.[12] He declared that the church was also silent about the destruction of the culture of his people and about the discrimination they suffered.

The Church was not totally silent about the injustices. But its statements aimed to please all sides. A California bishop said the Church supported the theories and concepts of social justice but did not align itself with "a particular union, owner organization, or other secular enterprise."[13] Bishop Humberto Medeiros of Brownsville defended union organization but in the same breath spoke of the right of "any other group of men who need to unite in order to protect and defend [themselves] against the unjust demands of management or labor."[14]

THE CHURCH AND THE FARMWORKERS

In 1949, four priests of the Archdiocese of San Francisco organized the Mission Band to serve farmworkers in California. Fathers Thomas McCullough, Donald McDonnell, John Garcia, and Ronald Burke convinced Archbishop John J. Mitty that the Church was not serving the hundreds of thousands of farmworkers in the state. Aspiring to be "priests of the poor," they traveled up and down the valleys of California for twelve years. As part of their ministry, they made farmworkers aware of the social doctrine of the Church and of their rights as workers. One of the leaders who benefited was Cesar Chavez, principal organizer of the United Farm Workers Union. He spent many nights discussing with Father McDonnell the teachings on the rights of labor. The education was mutual because the missioners also became aware of the injustices suffered by the workers.

The work of these priests brought into play the fundamental dilemma the Church always faces: support of the poor brings a confrontation with the rich. The growers soon began to question the right of the four priests to speak for the Church. In 1958 the growers, realizing they could not intimidate Mitty, started to pressure other bishops in California. They accused the priests of meddling in politics and suggested that the Church should not be exempt from taxation. In 1958 and 1959, many growers in the Stockton area sent the local bishop a signed statement to the effect that unless he pulled the priests out, "the Church should be registered as a lobbyist and denied tax-free status."[15] As a result the bishop of the Diocese of Fresno, Aloysius J. Willinger, denounced the priests of the Mission Band as leftists following the communist line. The bishop of San Diego, Charles F. Buddy, declared that it was not the proper role of the Mission Band to help the farmworkers organize to win social justice.

Mitty never gave in, but when he was terminally ill, in 1962, the chancellor of the San Francisco Archdiocese ended the Mission Band. The four priests were ordered to avoid further involvement in agricultural labor.

Nevertheless, the Mission Band established a pattern of service that was to be emulated in other areas. In Texas, when organizing activity began in 1966, two "outside" priests came to assist the workers: Father William Killian, executive director of the San Antonio archdiocesan weekly, and Father Sherrill Smith, social action director for the San Antonio Archdiocese. As in California, the growers called them intruders who did not speak for the Church. Bishop Medeiros of Brownsville asked Archbishop Lucey of San Antonio to withdraw them. Killian and Smith were ordered out of the Valley in 1967. Lucey sent them to New Mexico on a mandatory retreat and suspended four other priests who protested his action publicly.[16]

Protestants also forced the bishops to act. When Chavez and the farmworkers were finally able to go on strike in 1965 after Congress canceled the Bracero program, the California Migrant Ministry was the first church presence in the camps. Chavez asked: "Why do the Protestants come out here and help the people, demanding nothing and give all their time to serving the farmworkers while our own parish priests stay in their churches where few people come and feel uncomfortable?"[17] In response, Bishop Timothy Manning of Fresno appointed Father Mark Day as chaplain of the farmworkers.

The person most responsible for winning Church support was Cesar Chavez, himself. First, there was the unselfish witness of his own personal life. While leaders of other unions received huge salaries, he lived on $5 a week plus expenses, just like any other member of the union. He refused offers of well-salaried positions. He made sacrifice a reality in his own life. He emphasized that when a person sacrifices, he forces others to do the same. Giving a twist to the machismo of Hispanic culture, he said:

> When we are really honest with ourselves we must admit that our lives are all that really belong to us. So it is how we use our lives that determines what kind of men we are. It is my deepest belief that only by giving our lives do we find life. I am convinced that the truest test of courage, the strongest act of manliness is to sacrifice ourselves for others in totally non-violent struggle for justice. To be a man is to suffer for others. God help us to be men.

Second, Chavez organized the Church behind him by using religious symbols in his struggle. When the farmworkers, to present their grievances to the state legislature, marched hundreds of miles to Sacramento the banner of Our Lady of Guadalupe led the marchers. In 1968, he made a twenty-five day fast for peace and nonviolence, during which he lost thirty-five pounds. By the end, he was almost too weak to walk or talk.

But it was his commitment to nonviolence, the strongest feature of his spirituality, that finally swung the bishops, cautious as always, behind him. Chavez cultivated two ideals: the nonviolence of Jesus and the spirit of St. Francis of Assisi. He believed that the poor can be more powerful than the wealthy because there is nothing anyone can take from them.

In 1969, with an international grape boycott already in effect, the National Conference of Catholic Bishops refused to support the boycott. But they appointed an Ad Hoc Committee on Farm Labor: Bishops Joseph F. Donnelly of Hartford, chairman; Medeiros, of Brownsville; Hugh Donohue of Fresno, and Walter Curtis of Bridgeport, Connecticut. Monsignor George Higgins of the United States Catholic Conference was named consultant to the committee and Monsignor Roger Mahony as its secretary.[18]

Thanks to the mediation of the committee, within six months the United Farm Workers had nearly 100 contracts with grape growers. Then the bishops mediated a jurisdictional dispute with the Teamsters Union in the lettuce fields. But the growers and Teamster locals refused to abide by the agreements. Three years later, the grape growers refused to renegotiate with the UFW and the workers went out on strike again.

During the summer of 1973, the police arrested 4,000 persons, including 60 priests and religious. The protestors were challenging court injunctions they saw as prejudicial and unconstitutional. Many strikers, men and women, were beaten. On August 1, a shotgun blast from a passing truck wounded an 18-year-old man picketing at the Tudor ranch in Tulare County. Ten days later, shots fired from a field in the Missakian vineyards near Delano wounded Marcelina Barajas and Paul Salgado. The same day a car driven by a private policeman struck three pickets in Kern County. On August 16, a sniper shot 60-year-old Juan de La Cruz dead as he and his wife stood on the picket line at the Giumara vineyards. Two days later Nagi Mohsin Daifullah died after a deputy struck him on the head with a flashlight. In the face of such violence, Chavez suspended picketing and instituted a grape boycott which eventually brought the growers to the bargaining table again.

From its creation in 1969 to 1973, the Bishops' Committee on Farm Labor shed their neutrality. In 1973, Bishop Donnelly and Monsignor Higgins stood on the picket line with the farmworkers when growers in the Coachella Valley refused to sign new contracts. They were influenced by a decision by the California Supreme Court that the Teamsters had been in collusion with lettuce growers, by an attempt to pass Proposition 22, which was, in the words of Father Eugene Boyle of the National Federation of Priests Councils "extremely disenfranchising of the poor."[19] As a result of all this, the bishops voted to support the farmworkers' lettuce and grape boycotts.

The issue seemed to have been settled when the California legislature passed the Agricultural Labor Relations Act in 1975. Bishop Roger Mahony, recently promoted to auxiliary bishop of Fresno, headed the board appointed to mediate labor disputes. For a time, under a Democratic governor in Sacramento, the law worked well. But in the 1980s, a Republican governor, George Deukmejian, and a less sympathetic legislature, cut funding and the Act was poorly administered or not at all. The contracts of the UFW dwindled and unfavorable judgments in two lawsuits put financial strains on the union. Chavez instituted a new grape boycott but the public responded poorly. In 1988, Chavez underwent another long fast, which stirred only transient sympathy and commitment, leaving the future of the UFW in doubt.

Farmworker organizing had been even less successful in other states. In Arizona a right-to-work law blocked union organizing. In Texas, the violence of the Texas Rangers and other police forces and unconstitutional acts sanctioned by the courts defeated the farmworkers. In 1975, a melon grower, C. I. Miller of Hidalgo County, fired an automatic shotgun at striking workers, wounding eleven. Though he boasted publicly that he had "opened season" on them, a grand jury refused to indict him. Legislatures had not passed a similar law to the California Act, nor had Congress modified labor law to include farmworkers.

This sad condition was due to the political power of the growers and the indifference of the legislators.

URBAN STRUGGLES

The Church in the 1970s also became involved in the urban struggle of Hispanics, but in a less public way. Often it was only Hispanic clergy who took part. New Mexico priests took part in the marches and meetings of the Alianza Land Grants Movement of northern New Mexico. They also helped packing house workers in Albuquerque win better pay and working conditions, joined a coalition of Concerned Citizens for Better Education, and pushed for an end to discrimination in the judicial system in New Mexico.

In Denver the Church was ambivalent about the Crusade for Justice, founded in 1965 by a former high-ranking boxer-turned-politician, poet, and, ultimately, barrio leader—Rodolfo Corky Gonzales. The Crusade struggled against the dehumanization of urban life: schools with a semblance of jails, policemen who brutalized the innocent along with the guilty, businesses owned by outsiders that gouged residents of the barrios and other forms of discrimination. It supported students who walked out of schools protesting the remarks of a teacher who said Mexicans were stupid. Because Gonzales, unlike Cesar Chavez, did not espouse nonviolence, the Church was cautious. Nevertheless, the Archdiocese provided aid to the Crusade's Tlatelolco School, which sought to instill Hispanic values and culture, both denigrated in the city's schools. One year Archbishop James Casey came unannounced to the Crusade's Easter Mexican dinner, donated $100 to the building fund and urged those present to cherish their history and culture.

The most significant urban issue in which the Church played a crucial role was the strike that began on May 10, 1972, at the Farah Manufacturing Company. At that time Farah was the largest manufacturer of men's slacks in the nation, with plants in Albuquerque and Las Cruces in New Mexico and in El Paso, Victoria and San Antonio in Texas. The company president, William Farah, would not recognize the union the workers had elected to represent them. There were 10,400 employees, 85 percent of them Mexican American women earning an average weekly salary of $69. After the workers consulted with El Paso's Bishop Sydney Metzger, he became their chief advocate. When the strikers instituted a boycott of Farah slacks and jeans, Metzger wrote to every Catholic bishop in the country, expressing his support of the strike and endorsing the boycott.

With Metzger's support, a Mexican American priest, Jesse Muñoz, made his parish the headquarters of the strike. On Tuesday afternoons, the strikers had their weekly meeting at the Church. Weekly strike benefits and special relief checks for workers from Juarez, across the Rio Grande from El Paso, were passed out at the parish hall. Another priest, Donald Bauer, worked full-time with the union, the Amalgamated Clothing Workers of America.

Metzger and Muñoz were vilified by the Chamber of Commerce, the business community, and the local press. Some Protestant clergy campaigned for Farah but the Texas Conference of Churches endorsed the strike. Its efforts—and those of other bishops and Catholic clergy—helped cause a $10 million drop in sales for Farah in 1972 and another $10 million in 1973. The stock of the manufacturer fell from $30 to $8 a share. Farah closed plants, dismissed workers wholesale, but after 21 months the union won its struggle.

A more far-reaching service of the Church to Hispanics in urban areas was carried out through the Campaign for Human Development (CHD), the Church's anti-poverty program, begun in 1970. It contributed to many self-help projects or causes that made a significant difference in the lives of Hispanics. For example, in 1971 it gave $100,000 to PADRES to develop a mobile ministry team. In 1977, it gave a grant to the Mexican American Legal Defense and Educational Fund to seek voting rights for disenfranchised Mexican Americans. During that same period it helped Communities Organized for Public Service (COPS) to get started in San Antonio.

COPS

COPS began in 1973 when Ernie Cortez, a native of the city's West Side slums, fresh from training at Saul Alinsky's Industrial

Areas Foundation in Chicago, began knocking on doors looking for leaders with a following and with a network of communication. He found both in the parishes, the presidents of the Holy Name Society, the Ladies Guild or school PTA. Soon, too, the pastors and curates became involved. A tall, blunt young priest, Al Benavides, became the chief spokesperson for COPS. By then it was a federation of thirty-eight organizations from Catholic parishes and a scattering of Protestant churches based in the inner-city barrios of San Antonio.

COPS helped change the election system from at-large to single-district for city councilors. As a result, poor areas won political power they had previously lacked. Long neglected by city and county government, they soon won $100 million in needed improvements, such as storm drains, adequate water and sewers, street paving, and traffic lights at dangerous intersections. At the group's first annual convention, Bishop Patricio Flores told them:

> You are here today not as supplicants with downcast eyes, not as welfare recipients, not as beggars. You are here as equals, as responsible, law-abiding, tax-paying people. You are a people who with your sweat have helped shape this country, this state and particularly this city. You seek no special favor. You seek a just share of your tax monies to have a decent community. You have a right to equal and just consideration.

When he saw what COPS had accomplished for the poor in San Antonio, Bishop Juan Arzube urged the Campaign for Human Development to fund a similar group in East Los Angeles. There was opposition from Catholic Charities and a strong in-house battle ensued, finally decided in Arzube's favor by Cardinal Timothy Manning. Soon afterward, Ernie Cortez began organizing and, in time, United Neighborhoods Organization (UNO) was achieving impressive results. After Cortez had finished there, he moved on to Houston. Others began similar organizations in El Paso and in the Rio Grande Valley in Texas.

In the process of revitalizing the community, COPS did the same for the participating parishes. At St. Timothy's, where

Father Benavides was the pastor, Sunday Mass attendance went from 700 to 1,300 each Sunday. Lay leaders trained by COPS were soon improving and adding to the services offered by the parish: a new catechetical program, services to the elderly, a new liturgy that drew a citywide congregation. Social involvement, rather than conflicting with spiritual concerns, enhanced all aspects of the parish's programs.

At the same time, the Charismatic movement was revitalizing the spiritual life of many Hispanics. There are hundreds of Spanish-speaking prayer groups throughout the country. In the Los Angeles archdiocese alone, an estimated 60,000 belong in the movement, most of them of Mexican origin. Many are associated with Charisma in Missions, led by Marilynn Kramer, a former Assembly of God minister who became a convert to Catholicism. She said that Charisma in Missions touches the lives of more than 500,000 each year.[20] Hispanics find in the movement the warmth they experience in their popular religion. Though Los Angeles undoubtedly leads, the charismatic renewal is strong in many other areas. It is credited with keeping many Hispanics in the Catholic Church who might otherwise have joined Protestant denominations.

A strong beginning has also been made in the development of a theology to guide ministry for Hispanics. Father Virgil Elizondo gained wide acclaim for his reflections on religion and culture. He has lectured all over the world. A handful of others, following his lead, are developing a theology of the Hispanic experience. In 1988, Jesuit Father Allan Deck established the Academy of Hispanic Theologians at the Jesuit School of Theology at Berkeley. By mid-1989 it had identified eighty Hispanics eligible for membership and forty of them had already joined. Some Hispanics have won advanced degrees at prestigious divinity schools like Harvard, Princeton, and the Institut Catholique in Paris. Unfortunately, some of these men and women have not received the best teaching opportunities upon graduation and have had to settle for lesser jobs in ministry.

Recent years have also seen many developments in liturgy. The *Instituto de Liturgia Hispana* was organized at the Mexican American Cultural Center in the late seventies at the urging of Jesuit Father John Gallen. By 1989, it had a membership of about one hundred. It assists the Bishops' Committee on the Liturgy in its work. A Subcommittee on Hispanic Liturgy, headed in 1989 by Bishop Ricardo Ramirez, adapted many official texts for Spanish liturgy. The Northeast Pastoral Center put together the first Spanish-language lectionary for use among the Spanish-speaking in the United States.

In all these areas, the eighties have been a rich time for Hispanics.

—7—

The Church and Immigrants

THE CUBAN EXODUS

The Church in the United States has had a long interest in Hispanic immigration. As early as 1922, an office was established in El Paso to help the many Mexicans forced to immigrate because of the Mexican Revolution and its aftershocks. But the greatest effort all across the nation, especially in Florida, began in 1959 after Fidel Castro overthrew the Cuban dictator, Fulgencio Batista.

The first to come were 3,000 persons connected with the overthrown Batista regime. But by the end of the year about 64,000 had left. By the time of the Cuban missile crisis in 1962, they were joined by another 181,000 immigrants. Though most were from the middle and upper classes, one-fourth of the exiles came from blue-collar jobs.[1] During this time, because of fears that the government would take away the rights of parents, 14,048 children reached Miami without their parents.[2] For twenty months, the Catholic Service Bureau of Miami, headed by Msgr. Bryan O. Walsh, provided foster care, a task later assumed by the federal government.

From the Cuban missile crisis to 1965, only 55,916 came. But between then and 1971, under a program of family reunification, 297,318 more Cubans arrived. This was followed by another lull, shattered in 1980, when another 120,000 arrived in the boatlift from the port of Mariel. In all 875,000 left Cuba.

While 10 percent of the inhabitants in pre-Castro Cuba were practicing Catholics, as many as 80 percent of the first 100,000 arriving in 1960-61 fit that description as opposed to two percent of those on the Mariel boatlift.[3] The first refugees were almost exclusively whites; the Mariel group was 65 percent black. Overall, 35.3 percent of the immigrants (exclusive of those on the Mariel boat lift) were blue-collar workers.[4] Among the exiles were 135 priests, 49 of whom went to work in the Archdiocese of Miami.

Many adjustments were made by the Church in Miami to minister to the Cubans. Priests were sent to Puerto Rico to study language and culture. By the end of 1962, seven parishes had special Masses with sermons in Spanish. By 1966, there were eight Spanish-speaking priests, with sixteen parishes offering Mass in Spanish. In the first months of the exodus, $1 million was spent by the church to help the immigrants and, even though the federal Cuban Refugee Emergency Assistance Program (enacted in 1961) was contributing the bulk of the assistance, that amount had grown to $2.5 million by 1965. *The Voice*, the diocesan paper, began a Spanish column in 1959 and later expanded it to a special section with its own staff.[5] In 1988, *La Voz*, the Spanish edition of the diocesan paper, had a circulation of about 25,000.

As a result of the Cuban influx, two high schools for boys and one for girls were established in 1961. They were staffed by priests, Sisters, and Brothers from Cuba. Bilingual programs became an integral part of the curriculum of the Catholic schools, where 45 percent of the students were Spanish-speaking by 1975. Eleven new parishes were established to serve the refugees. Spanish-speaking associate directors and staff members were appointed to major departments of the chancery. The archdiocesan seminary became bilingual and bicultural, a model for the rest of the nation. By the end of 1980, Hispanics comprised 39 percent of the population of metropolitan Miami. Estimates of the number of Catholics ranged from 500,000 to 850,000, with Hispanics accounting for 63 percent and Haitians seven percent.

Two Cuban priests had been ordained bishops by 1988, Agustin Roman, auxiliary in Miami, and Enrique San Pedro, a Jesuit who is auxiliary in the Diocese of Galveston-Houston. Father Mario Vizcaino became director of the Southeast Regional Office for Hispanics and also of the Southeast Pastoral Center.

Msgr. Orlando Fernandez was vicar for the Hispanics. Father Felipe Estevez served several years as rector of the seminary. Father Raul Del Valle, who died in 1988, was the chancellor of the Archdiocese of New York. A Cuban layman, Jose Debasa, was appointed finance director of the Archdiocese of Los Angeles by Archbishop Roger Mahony.

THE PUERTO RICAN MIGRATION

Between 1950 and 1960, the Puerto Rican population living on the mainland went from 300,000 to 887,000. By 1970, it had increased to 1.4 million people of Puerto Rican birth or parentage. The exodus was so great that it was comparable to fifty million leaving the United States to settle elsewhere. It affected most families. One cause was the decline of agriculture in Puerto Rico. From 1940 to 1970, the number of farm jobs dropped from 230,000 to 74,000.[6] Moreover, society offered little opportunity for upward mobility. Real unemployment was several times more than on the mainland. In 1970 it was nearly 30 percent.[7] The mainland offered more job opportunities and at better pay than in Puerto Rico. But in times of recession in the United States, as in the early 1970s, the migration actually reversed.

The Puerto Ricans are poorer than any other Hispanic group in the nation; in 1986 their family income was $12,000 less than that of Cubans, the wealthiest Hispanic group, and $5,000 less than that of Mexican Americans. Puerto Rican median family income was $14,584 as opposed to $19,326 for Mexican Americans and $26,770 for Cubans. Among Hispanics, Puerto Ricans bear more of the signs of an underclass. From 1956 to 1976, out-of-wedlock births among Puerto Ricans in the United States rose from eleven percent to forty-six percent.[8] Among Hispanics, Puerto Ricans have the highest percentage (43.3) of female-headed households with no husband present.[9]

Arriving on the mainland at a time when national parishes were no longer in vogue and without their own priests to minister to them, Puerto Ricans suffered as much, or perhaps more, bigotry and intolerance as any other group. Twenty-five years after the zenith of the migration in the 1950s, they had few vocations. "We have three native Puerto Rican priests in this country that I know of," Pablo Sedillo, director of the Secretariat for Hispanics, said in the mid-1970s. "There are very few Puerto Ricans in seminaries studying for the priesthood or the religious life."[10] Because this group was fleeing neither political nor religious persecution, there was much less interest in helping them settle. Moreover, the political benefit evident in the Cuban resettlement was missing.

There were, however, some optimistic notes. The New York Archdiocese already had an office for the Hispanic apostolate by the early 1960s. As previously mentioned, the *Cursillo* was introduced soon after it came to the United States and it proved an effective tool for renewal. Many priests and seminarians were sent to Ponce, Puerto Rico, to study Spanish. About 400 English-speaking priests eventually learned some Spanish and became familiar with the culture.[11]

THE MEXICAN MIGRATION

The Bracero program, instituted during World War II to deal with a labor shortage, brought more and more of these seasonal workers in the postwar period. In its peak year, 1956, a total of 445,197 labored throughout the nation. At the same time, however, there were more workers available than the Bracero program accepted. Hundreds of thousands crossed the border during that period. By then other industries had seen the value of the cheap labor Mexicans could provide. Many of these worked in the garment industry, in hotels as maids, in restaurants as busboys and dishwashers, in affluent residential areas as servants and gardeners and in thousands of other sweatshop firms.

Following the pattern established in the 1920s and 1930s, the Immigration and Naturalization Service (INS) carried out a massive deportation in the early 1950s. Counting those apprehended as they tried to enter the United States illegally, "Operation Wetback" expelled 3.8 million in the course of several years. Afterward, the INS boasted in its 1955 annual report: "The so-called 'wetback' problem no longer exists. . . . The border has been secured." But by 1973, the INS found it necessary to begin more mass roundups, which continued on a sporadic basis into the 1980s.

In 1964 Congress canceled the Bracero program by refusing to renew Public Law 78, the authority under which it was carried out. But illegal immigration or migration (some experts insist most Mexicans come only to work temporarily) increased dramatically. The year the Bracero program was canceled, only 43,844 persons were apprehended at the border for trying to enter without permission. By 1977, such arrests had increased to 954,778.[12] In the 1980s, more than a million were turned away each year. The tradition going back to the 1880s of coming to work in the U. S. could not be nullified simply by canceling the Bracero program. A study made in the 1970s showed that many of the illegals then had fathers who had been Braceros.[13]

Meanwhile, conditions in Mexico were forcing more and more workers north. The country had too many people for the arable land available. Unemployment and underemployment in Mexico in 1977 was 30 percent.[14] Not just lack of employment but of well-paid jobs stimulated the migration. At the same time, inflation was rampant. Successive devaluations in the 1970s and 1980s created a bigger gap between earning power in Mexico and in the U. S., even at minimum wage levels. The result was an unprecedented flow of workers across the border.

In the United States, this phenomenon was expressed in terms of an invasion by former Marine General Leonard Chapman, who was commissioner of immigration from 1973 to 1977. He toured the country warning that the illegals, whom he estimated to number as many as 12 million, could bring catastrophe to the country. Though other experts declared that many Mexicans came only for six months to a year and that the number of these workers did not exceed four or five million, Chapman's views caused public alarm and rising violence along the border. Polls showed that as high as 82 percent of the American people favored rounding up the illegals and sending them back. The Ku Klux Klan offered to place its own patrols along the border.

The Church was slow to develop a coherent position. It opposed illegal immigration and the Bracero program in its later stages because it thought that would enable the domestic farmworkers to organize. That position, however, was not consistent with Church doctrine that there is a prior natural right of persons to immigrate when there is a need.[15] In the ensuing debate over illegal immigration, Catholics more often voiced the view that the nation had a right to sovereignty over its borders.

Despite such ambivalence, the Church did speak out on occasion when the rights of immigrants were violated. In 1976, an Arizona rancher and his two sons were accused of kidnaping and torturing three workers who had entered the country illegally. In 1979, due to pressure by a coalition that included Hispanics, the United States Catholic Conference (USCC) and individual Catholic clergy, religious women, and laity, the sons were indicted — the father had died in the meantime — and one of them was convicted after a state trial and two federal trials.

Among the bishops, Roger Mahony of Stockton (Calif.) and Patricio Flores of San Antonio were particularly active in opposing violence against the illegal workers. Mahony, when he was the ordinary of the Diocese of Stockton, once led a procession of hundreds of persons to the local offices of the Immigration and Naturalization Service (INS). Throughout the years Church personnel frequently served on advisory committees of the U.S. Commission on Civil Rights dealing with immigration problems.

NEW REFUGEES

Meanwhile, new refugees from Central America have joined the flow. Over the past few decades, large communities of Salvadorans, Guatemalans, and Nicaraguans, fleeing war and political repression, established themselves in San Francisco, Los Angeles, New York, and Washington, D. C. In the 1980s, with the Reagan Administration's decision to seek military solutions to the problems of Central America, the exodus increased. Over a few years, hundreds of thousands of new refugees arrived. INS detention centers formerly filled with Mexican illegals were now housing Central Americans. The Administration took the position that they didn't qualify under the 1980 Refugee Act, which defined refugees as persons forced to flee because of fear or the actual experience of persecution. Administration officials claimed that the Central Americans came for economic reasons.

Though the Church was deeply involved in trying to help the

refugees, the bishops took the cautious position of opposing the war and speaking about rights without openly supporting those priests, religious men and women, and laity willing to risk prosecution by providing concrete assistance. Even the Hispanic bishops, who might have chosen a prophetic role, remained largely on the sidelines. The risks were taken by poor Hispanic families in the barrios along the Rio Grande, a few priests and nuns throughout the nation, as well as some Protestant and Jewish clergy and laity. Barrio residents, parishes, and religious orders provided hospitality when the refugees came to their doors. Some religious orders and societies contributed to pay for the legal services to win political asylum for the refugees.

In El Paso, Annunciation House, a house of hospitality established by a layman, Ruben Garcia, took in anyone who knocked on the door. Along the border, the most courageous bishop was John Fitzpatrick of Brownsville. He supported Casa Oscar Romero, which at one time housed 500 refugees. Bishop Raymundo Peña of El Paso provided the building Garcia used for Annunciation House. But Bishop Rene Gracida of Corpus Christi, when asked to comment after one of his pastors was arrested and charged with transporting refugees to the interior, was quoted in the press as saying the priest had made an error in judgment.

Eventually, in the 1980s, some religious congregations and parishes declared themselves sanctuaries for the refugees. Claretian Father Luis Olivares, pastor of Our Lady Queen of Angels in Los Angeles, opened the church every night so that scores of refugees could sleep in the pews. Father Michael Kennedy, a Jesuit, ran the parish's refugee center. Jesuits at Dolores Mission and at several houses sheltered refugees. Similar efforts were made by parishes in the Diocese of Rockville Centre on Long Island, New York.

In Tucson and across the Mexican border, several Protestant churches and Catholic parishes joined together to provide sanctuary. The leaders of this effort were indicted and tried on various charges. While the trial was going on in federal court in Tucson, the Bishops' Committee for Hispanic Affairs was meeting in a retreat house nearby, getting an orientation on the pastoral plan voted upon by the Third National Encuentro.

Meanwhile, the defendants were fighting for their freedom in federal court downtown. None of the bishops visited the courtroom to show their solidarity with the defendants.

On November 5, 1986, Congress passed the Immigration Reform and Control Act, a law that had been debated for years. Its aim was to enable the U. S. to regain control of its borders by stopping the flow of illegals. To do that it became a crime for employers to hire them. At the same time, Congress made those who could prove they had entered the country prior to January 1, 1982, eligible for an amnesty that would eventually lead to citizenship. While the USCC had opposed employer sanctions, the bishops as a group did not oppose the law because they favored the amnesty program. Between May 5, 1987 and May 4, 1988, 1.8 million refugees applied for amnesty. The Migration and Refugee Services Department of the USCC and many dioceses cooperated with the INS in bringing the illegals in to apply for the amnesty. Roger Mahony, by then promoted to Archbishop of Los Angeles, cooperated most closely with the INS in the legalization effort. He said the Church should assist as many as possible to win amnesty and then seek to change the law to include those who had been left out: refugees and other persons who entered the country without permission after 1982. The law, however, led to widespread discrimination against citizens or legal immigrants who appeared foreign (i.e. Hispanics and Asians). In November 1988, the bishops at their annual meeting in Washington approved a statement expressing their opposition to employer sanctions. But it was unclear whether, having gone along with the law in 1986, their voice would have much effect now.

Immigrants provide much of the Hispanic leadership in the Church. Ten of the twenty-one Hispanic bishops in the United States are immigrants: two from Mexico, two from Cuba, two from Spain, two from Puerto Rico,[16] one from Ecuador and one from Venezuela. Most of the remainder are the sons of immigrants. Of some 1,954 Hispanic priests in the United States, fewer than 200 are native born. The proportion of native-born among the 1,300 Sisters and Brothers is similar. Furthermore, most seminarians are immigrants or the sons of immigrants.

Many important offices in the Church are headed by Hispanic

immigrants. For example, Mario Paredes, a Chilean, heads the Northeast Regional Office for Hispanics; Father Mario Vizcaino, a Cuban, the Southeast Regional Office; Father Ricardo Chavez, son of Mexican immigrants, the West Coast office. Araceli Cantero, a Spaniard, is the editor of *La Voz*, the highly successful Spanish edition of the diocesan newspaper of the Archdiocese of Miami; Julio Alejandro Escalona, a Mexican, edits the Spanish edition of the *Chicago Catholic*. That pattern holds throughout the rest of the nation.

Traditionally, immigrants have revitalized the Church in the United States. Hispanics are no exception.

—8—

Hispanic American Protestantism in the United States

by Edwin E. Sylvest, Jr.

A history of the Hispanic church in the United States would be incomplete without a chapter on those who have joined Protestant denominations. Since it is appropriate that this history should be written by a Protestant, I asked Dr. Edwin E. Sylvest, Jr., a faculty member of the Perkins School of Theology at Southern Methodist University, to write this chapter.

Though the overwhelming majority of Hispanics are Catholics, Protestants — mainline as well as evangelical and pentecostal groups — have always presented a challenge. Particularly in the 1980s, though a time of greater ecumenical understanding, Catholic bishops have been alarmed at the accelerating rate of conversion of Hispanics to Protestant churches: about 60,000 a year. As of 1990, four million out of the twenty million Hispanics in the U. S. are members of Protestant denominations. Father Andrew Greeley, a sociologist, has called this "an ecclesiastical failure of unprecedented proportions."

Failure of the Catholic Church to minister adequately to its Hispanic members is seen as an important cause of conversions. Catholics feel that Protestant churches, typically with small congregations, are more hospitable and build a stronger sense of community. Furthermore, they offer ministers who are from the people themselves, i.e., Hispanics. The approach of these churches, particularly that of the evangelicals, is considered more affective, perhaps better attuned to Hispanic culture.

Nevertheless, as Sylvest's essay suggests, the experience of Hispanic Protestants has not been as happy as some Catholics imagine. While proportionately more have been able to take part in ordained ministry, they have occupied, throughout this period, the same second-class status that may have led them to leave the Catholic Church.

— *Moises Sandoval*

A CONQUERED PEOPLE: PROTESTANT RESPONSE (1821-98)

Texas was the place where Protestant Christianity and Hispanic culture made initial contact within the present limits of the United States. Anglo settlers began making their way into Texas and Coahuila, a frontier province of New Spain, in the waning years of the second decade of the nineteenth century. After Mexico became an independent nation in 1821, the government encouraged colonization in Texas and Coahuila. Stephen F. Austin and his colony of San Felipe were among the first Anglos to benefit from Mexican immigration policy.

Although Anglo colonists were required officially to become Roman Catholic, Protestant practice was tolerated. As a result Protestant missionaries traveled freely, preaching to the burgeoning Anglo population. By 1933 Baptists, Methodists, and Cumberland Presbyterians had established congregations and erected church buildings. Any Protestant ministry to Mexicans was coincidental to serving the religious needs of Anglo colonists who were culturally Protestant, if not actively participating church people. During this period the normative pattern of Protestant outreach to Mexicans was through distribution of the Scriptures. In 1833 Sumner Bacon, a Cumberland Presbyterian minister, was commissioned a colporteur of the American Bible Society, supplying Spanish Bibles until his death in 1844. David Ayres, a Methodist layperson, undertook a similar ministry during the same period. Both discovered great interest in the Bible among the Spanish-speaking population, notwithstanding the opposition of Roman Catholic priests to its distribution. Some were eager to purchase the book.[1]

With the independence of Texas in 1836 came greater freedom for missionary activity among the Spanish-speaking. Protestant mission boards and churches, however, continued to be interested primarily in the Anglos. Efforts with Hispanics were regarded as tactics in a larger strategy of missionary activity in Mexico. Robert Blair, the first Protestant missionary officially assigned to work with Spanish-speaking persons, viewed his work as an opportunity to learn the language so that he might undertake to enlighten the "semi-heathen, semi-Catholics who use the Spanish language in Mexico."[2]

Blair established a school, Aranama College, to train Mexican youth for missionary work in their native land. The college was short-lived but the concept endured well into the present century as a primary means of missionary outreach to Mexico, and eventually to Mexican Americans.

Allowing for good intention and sincere motivation, it is nonetheless evident that the ministry of Protestant churches during this contact period was an instrument of marginalization. A people already victimized by changing political and economic systems suffered the further insult of being of only secondary importance to the religious establishment of Anglo settlers. Lack of comprehensive planning was due not to respect and concern for the development of a more adequate Roman Catholic ministry (that was badly needed) but to the insidious racism and ethnocentrism that unfortunately characterized the Anglo Saxon Protestant ethos of the United States.

THE NEW SOUTHWEST (1846-69)

Though war with Mexico interrupted missionary activity in Texas, the resolution of the conflict through the Treaty of Guadalupe Hidalgo created a much larger field. Mexico lost half of its territory and the population centers in New Mexico and California. Mexicans who chose not to "remove" to the Republic of Mexico became citizens of the United States, Hispanic Americans. But though "regeneration" of native peoples had figured importantly as justification for the war and annexation of territory, Methodists, Baptists, and Presbyterians who began almost immediately to work in New Mexico and California focused their interest primarily on the English-speaking population. Attention toward Spanish-speaking peoples was focused on Mexico. Returning soldiers spoke of the "moral destitution" of a land never penetrated by "pure Christianity."

Melinda Rankin, a young New England Presbyterian, saw that defeated Mexicans needed to respond:

> Our country had conquered them and subjugated them to its own terms; and was there nothing more demanded for this bleeding, riven and desolated country? Were there no hearts to commiserate the helpless condition of these perishing millions of souls under the iron heel of papal power, with all its soul destroying influences? I could not avoid the impression that an important duty devolved upon Evangelical Christendom to try to do something for the moral elevation of this people who had so long been sitting in the region of the shadow of death.[3]

Rankin established a school for girls in Brownsville, Texas, and distributed Bibles. Both efforts reduplicated the patterns already established in Texas by Bacon and Ayers, and both efforts were primarily aimed at Mexico, where Rankin went in 1851.

Though only of secondary interest, Mexican Americans began to respond. They were especially interested in the Bible and read it avidly as it became available. In New Mexico, where the Methodist Episcopal Church appointed a missionary in 1853, the Bible brought the first recorded convert to Protestantism. Ambrosio Gonzales reported: "It was to me a new book. I read until the chickens were crowing for day. I lay down on the lounge in the same room and soon fell asleep. When I woke the sun was shining through the window into my face. The Sun of Righteousness was shining brightly in my soul. I have been a Christian and a Protestant ever since."[4]

Gonzales became a Methodist class leader in Peralta, where

in sixteen years (1855-71) he developed a class of 42 persons. Lay leadership exemplified by Gonzales was strengthened as the first Hispanic Americans became members of the clergy. In 1853 a dissident Roman Catholic priest became the first ordained Protestant clergyman in the newly acquired territories. He preached his first sermon as a Protestant on the Plaza in Santa Fe on November 20, 1853.

Some Hispanic Americans, eager to assimilate into the life of the new nation, converted to Protestant Christianity. The churches were pleased to count them among their members but failed to entrust them with significant institutional leadership. Anglo missionaries and pastors supervised their work. An internal colony of the United States was being formed and the churches, Roman Catholic and Protestant, were part of the process.

MISSIONARY RENEWAL AND INSTITUTIONAL GROWTH (1869-89)

The Civil War disrupted missionary activity among Hispanics but a resurgence occurred after the conflict ended. The story of Alejo Hernandez illustrates the complex and conflicting forces in Hispanic American Protestantism during this period.[5] Hernandez, a Catholic seminarian in Mexico when the French set out to establish the Austrian Maximilian as Emperor of Mexico, left the seminary in 1862, disgusted with the support the hierarchy gave the imperial experiment. Joining the liberal army of Benito Juarez, Hernandez was captured by the French and eventually crossed the Rio Bravo (the Mexican name for the Rio Grande) in 1869 in search of a Spanish Bible.

While in northern Mexico, Hernandez had acquired one of many tracts the American Tract Society asked soldiers of General Zachary Taylor to distribute to the local population during their invasion of Mexico in 1846. It was a piece of nativistic propaganda entitled *Evenings with the Romanists* whose frequent reference to Scripture motivated Hernandez to search for a vernacular text of the Bible.

One day while walking in Brownsville, Hernandez was lured by congregational singing into a small Protestant church.

Although he could not speak English, he was so moved that he went to the altar at the close of the service and dedicated himself to God. But when he returned to Mexico and attempted a ministry, he experienced such persecution and frustration that he came back to Texas. In Corpus Christi in 1871, he was licensed to preach by the Methodist Episcopal Church, South, ordained a deacon, and appointed to do missionary work among Hispanics in Texas.

But since Methodists were eager to develop their work in Mexico, Alejo Hernandez was appointed to begin a ministry in Mexico City. Failing health caused him to return to Corpus Christi, where he died in 1875. His work opened the possibility of developing Hispanic leadership for Spanish-speaking Protestantism in Texas.

While Anglo leadership continued in the development of Hispanic American Protestantism, an important milestone had been reached. Alexander Sutherland, Thomas Harwood, Henry Pratt, Una Roberts Lawrence, among others, played important roles, but so did Jose Policarpo Rodriguez, Santiago Tafolla, Trinidad Armendariz, Jose Maria Botello. Though missionary Protestantism would prevail for another half-century, Hispanic American Protestantism was achieving its own voice, though it was muted.

In the effort to develop Hispanic American clergy, the Protestant churches established a lower standard of preparation. Academic requirements deemed important for Anglo ministers were regarded as unnecessary for Spanish-speakers to serve their own people. Their curriculum was essentially a concentrated course in the Scriptures. It was felt that to do more would elevate Hispanic ministers beyond their prospective parishioners and create barriers. Furthermore, if pastors were not encouraged to achieve a fully comprehensive education, they would not be lured into secular occupations.[6] The pattern of undertrained, underpaid clergy, dependent upon Anglo patronage, was established.

Membership increased, clergy developed, institutional structures were formed and grew, but Hispanic Americans were relegated to secondary status in their own churches. Their Anglo patrons deemed it to be in the interest of the mission.

The essential patterns and structures of Hispanic American Protestantism in the Southwest were fixed in the years 1869-90. Anglos retained control of the churches and their institutions. Instead of building self-determination, the schools assured assimilation and accommodation to the customs and institutional interests of the conquering culture. Training of indigenous leaders was generally an expedient rather than an affirmation of the values and gifts of the other culture.

NEW PEOPLE, NEW MINISTRIES (1890-1930)

Increased immigration from Mexico beginning in the 1880s and peaking in the 1920s created new challenges for the churches in the Southwest.

After the imperialist war with Spain in 1898, the Hispanic populations of Cuba, Puerto Rico, and the Philippines became important areas of missionary endeavor. Indeed, concern for mission among those peoples was part of the ethos that led the United States to occupy those territories. New ties led to significant emigration from the islands, adding to the Cuban and Puerto Rican exiles already living in the United States prior to the war. Cuban enclaves in Tampa, Key West, and Miami experienced Protestant missionary activity. After the Cuban Revolution in 1959, many Cuban pastors came as refugees who served their own as well as other Hispanic communities.

The cultural ethos of these Caribbean immigrants was somewhat different from that of Mexicans and other Hispanics in the Southwest. Among the immigrants were Protestants who had responded to missionary activity in their homelands. Especially in Cuba and Puerto Rico, Protestant missionary activity had been undertaken by exiles who had returned home with their own new-found faith.[7]

For some, Protestantism represented the ideal of liberty and democracy associated with the struggle for independence on the islands, and for reform in Mexico. In both instances, the Roman Catholic Church was perceived as reactionary and an obstacle to desired transformation. Those attitudes were exploited and reinforced by some Protestant missionaries. As in the case of Alejo Hernandez in Texas, resentment against the hierarchy was reinforced by nativist sentiment in the United States and helped to develop strong anti-Catholic feeling among the immigrants. Such attitudes alienated some Protestant Hispanics from important elements of their own cultural heritage. In a nation that tended to welcome their labor but not them or their cultural traditions, many Hispanic Protestants were further alienated within their own communities.[8]

Response to the needs for service characterized much of the Protestant ministry during the years of the Mexican Revolution and World War I. The mainline Protestant churches developed schools and community centers. Besides adding to the congregational rolls, the immigrant population provided new leaders as well. From among the immigrants came persons with the education facilitating leadership development in the institutional life of the churches.

In southern California, where Hispanics were expanding rapidly, much of the impetus was to "Americanize" the Mexicans. Anglo Protestants worried that abysmal living and working conditions would lead the immigrants to opt for other political alternatives. As Presbyterian and Methodist executives saw it, the "question which is to be decided in the next few years is whether they [the Mexicans] are to be won to anarchy or Americanism; to Bolshevism or to democracy; to Trotsky or Christ."[9]

Not all concern for Americanization was motivated by the presumed socialist threat. Some Protestants felt a genuine, if paternalistic, desire to train men and women helping to develop the country. "Cut out the Mexicans and you cut out a large factor in our industries. Educate them and you add a sound and useful aid to our country's development, especially here in the Southwest."[10] Mexicans had, after all, built railroads, worked in the development of mines and the steel industry, and were engaged in producing food.

Despite such concern for the well-being of Mexican Americans, the churches did not resist the mistreatment of those repatriated during the Depression. Many Mexicans, welcomed when their services were needed, were sent "back where they came from." Many native-born Americans, especially those without documents, were deported too. Pastoral care and social services did not address the systemic marginalization of Hispanics in the U. S.

INSTITUTIONAL SUCCESS AND POPULAR CHALLENGE (1930-89)

This period saw the development of a new concept of community-based Christian ministry that addressed the needs of the whole person. "Houses of Neighborliness" and community centers became so important in some communities that the people began to regard them as "theirs" and to "secularize" them. Neighborhood priorities displaced the evangelistic emphases and strained relationships with the churches that conceived the centers as places where evangelization, if not proselytism, might occur.

Sponsoring denominational agencies, which were often related to churches committed to the growing movement of Protestant ecumenism, found it difficult to employ the neighborhood facilities in their evangelistic strategies because ecumenical ministries involved Roman Catholics in forming policy for the centers. Many centers were allowed to become relatively independent secular agencies.

Anglo sponsors as well as many "pietistic" Hispanic congregations, offended by the social activism of the centers, resisted the success of these ministries. That resistance became increasingly evident during the sixties when Hispanics displayed great ambivalence toward many of the activities of *La Raza*.

The tensions in the community-center ministries signaled an awareness that systemic issues would need to be addressed if the hopes of Hispanic immigrants were to be realized, and if justice for the entire Hispanic American community were to be achieved. Service-oriented ministries met needs that certainly required attention, but they did not create communities of reciprocity. Indeed, when reciprocity was achieved, enabling Hispanic Americans to participate in making policy, the service ministries became problematic for their sponsors.

The Hispanic American community itself saw the challenge to traditional structures as a threat. For some the issue was that of the church's proper relationship to the world and a concept of salvation that envisioned human fulfillment and final justice as eschatological hopes. For others, a challenge to the system compromised long-held dreams and hard-won institutional successes. By the mid-thirties some Hispanic Americans had received formal theological education, had been ordained as their Anglo counterparts, and had been appointed to positions of major responsibility within their denominational structures. There was reason to hope that shared power and responsibility would replace dependence and patronage.

In the Methodist church, Hispanics carried leadership responsibility and authority in conference structures. In the Texas Mexican Conference, predecessor of the Rio Grande Annual Conference, Alfredo Nañez, the first Hispanic American Methodist to complete his formal theological education with the B.D. degree from Southern Methodist University, and Francisco Ramos were named Presiding Elders. In similar fashion a Latin American Provisional Conference was established in southern California in 1941. Although in both cases Hispanic leaders worked under Anglo bishops and mission executives, they enjoyed significant autonomy in decision-making and administration.[11]

Many Hispanic Americans who served in the military during World War II began to envision full and equal participation in U.S. institutions, including the churches. Many felt that complete assimilation into the Anglo mainstream would bring greater benefit from the economic and political systems, a dream shared by Anglos too. The decision of the U.S. Supreme Court in *Brown vs. The Board of Education* developed widespread impetus to eliminate segregation, which existed in the churches as well as in the civil society. Presbyterians in Texas ended the Texas Mexican Presbytery and merged its congregations into other presbyteries. The Methodist Latin American Provisional Conference in California was also integrated into other structures.

Uncritical Anglo idealism, Hispanic desire for full participation, and economic opportunity all contributed to decisions to integrate. Unfortunately, the Hispanic Americans and others were expected to adopt the culture of the Anglo majority. Hispanic Americans and Anglos were to be equal participants, but in an Anglo system. Some Presbyterians in Texas refused to integrate on that basis and attempted to form an independent Spanish-speaking Protestant church. They failed for lack of resources and adequate leadership.[12]

Many Hispanic Methodists in California viewed the decision to integrate their conference as a defeat, but the Anglos prevailed. While some ministers were pleased with the economic advantage they gained through improved salaries, the laity saw no advantage in the new arrangement; they experienced isolation and rejection. Hispanic membership began to decline. By the late 1980s the principle of autonomy and the need to affirm cultural and linguistic values had been reinstituted with the establishment of a Latin American Mission District within the California-Pacific Annual Conference. The first Hispanic American bishop in the United Methodist Church, Elias Galvan, was elected in 1984 by the Western Jurisdiction that includes California.

In Texas and New Mexico the Rio Grande Conference, which was established in 1939 when Methodist Episcopal churches of the South and the North merged with the Methodist Protestant Church to become the Methodist Church, resisted pressures to merge with Anglo conferences. Although it needs economic help from the denomination, the Rio Grande Conference has developed strong Hispanic leadership that contributes to the national church and to the development of ministries within the region.

The use of Spanish and an appreciation of the cultural heritage are important elements of the self-understanding of the Rio Grande Conference, but because many of the younger members no longer speak Spanish, ministers in full-connection must be bilingual and practice bilingual worship in many congregations. That very bilingualism, so important to the new *mestizaje* of Hispanic Americans in an historically predominant Anglo society, may be the reason why mainline churches, with the exception of the Southern Baptists, show little or no growth in total membership at a time when Hispanics are the fastest growing group in the country. Much of that growth occurs in the most marginated sectors of the Hispanic community, sectors where bilingualism may be a requirement of the workplace but not in the household or the neighborhood.

As the Hispanic population in the nation grows and Anglo conferences and churches begin to respond with ministries, the Rio Grande Conference finds at once a major resource in developing those ministries and a target for severe criticism because its concepts of ministry do not always mirror the perceptions of Anglo decision-makers. The growing awareness of the need for Hispanic ministry brings with it controversy and threat. The United Methodist General Conference of 1988, responding to the petition of MARCHA, the Hispanic caucus, created a quadrennial study commission to develop a comprehensive plan for Hispanic ministry throughout the whole church. Similar efforts have been made by Presbyterians, Lutherans, and others.

One of the earliest and most comprehensive efforts to respond to Hispanics in the United States was undertaken by the United Presbyterian Church in response to the leadership of Jorge Lara-Braud in the sixties. Ironically, that action by the General Assembly came as Hispanics were becoming a less significant element than they were a decade earlier.

Southern Baptist mission agencies have been particularly effective in developing Hispanic ministries. Among traditional Protestant churches, the Southern Baptists probably have the largest Hispanic membership. They permit a degree of local autonomy that facilitates flexibility in responding to the needs and interests of particular congregations, though Hispanic churches appear to be well assimilated into denominational structures, problematic as they are for all Southern Baptists.

Efforts by mainline Hispanic Protestants to sustain strong denominational affiliations have affected pastoral responses to issues of social justice. In some cases Anglo congregations have responded more directly than the Hispanics.

There was no evident response, however, by either Anglo or Hispanic Protestants during the Zoot Suit riots of the forties. While the city of Los Angeles watched passively and Methodist Hispanics were preoccupied with making the Latin American Provisional Conference an effective instrument of ministry, Mexican American young people struggling to discover and express their identity were brutalized by United States naval personnel on leave and also by the police. Although the struggle of the Methodists and young people was the same, that is, to assert a cultural and personal identity different from that of the Anglo majority, neither group saw the other as an ally. Indeed the young people were viewed by Hispanic Protestants as social outcasts. The distance was great between organized Protestantism and "the first people to call themselves Chicanos."[13]

PROTESTANTISM AND SOCIAL PROTEST

As the Chicano movement developed during the 1960s, the distance between it and the churches narrowed in some respects, though it continued to be problematic. Hispanic American Reies Lopez Tijerina, a Pentecostal minister, led the struggle to recover lost land grants in northern New Mexico; Rodolfo "Corky" Gonzales, a member of the Presbyterian Church, led the urban struggle in Denver. The Migrant Ministry of the National Council of Churches was an early supporter of Cesar Chavez and his farmworkers.

There was, however, little or no participation of the churches as institutions. Though individual Hispanic Protestants, lay and clergy, took part in the struggle, few Hispanic congregations ventured forward. Most Hispanic church people reacted as the Anglos did. They were thoroughly integrated into an economic system governed by the interests of agribusiness.[14] As the struggle moved to Texas some Rio Grande pastors did take great risk to support the farmworkers and the Conference eventually adopted a resolution supporting the United Farmworkers boycott, but there was great ambivalence in the churches and little enthusiasm for serious and sustained engagement in the struggle.

Individual congregations on the frontier and in the cities have responded significantly to the crisis occasioned by the passage of the Immigration Reform and Control Act of 1986. Many Hispanic congregations have helped Central American refugees though it appears that none have taken formal action declaring themselves part of the Sanctuary movement. Response to concrete human need is easier than grappling with the politics of transformation on the larger issues of immigration and foreign policy, although Hispanic caucuses and leaders have helped formulate responses.

PENTECOSTALISM

If the slowly growing social consciousness and the implications of Christian faith represent one aspect of popular Protestantism, the phenomenon of Pentecostalism represents another. Though the two movements are frequently in conflict and seem mutually exclusive to many Hispanic Protestants, they do arise from common roots in the life experience of the people as in the Christian gospel itself. If the two movements converge in congregational life and denominational institutions, Hispanic Protestantism may emerge as a force to be reckoned with in U.S. society.

As in the general population, evangelical Christianity has become the most rapidly growing and vigorous movement within Protestantism. (There is also a significant charismatic movement within the Roman Catholic Church.) In the Hispanic American population, evangelicalism, especially Pentecostalism, is growing fast, a trend also seen in Latin America where Pentecostalism in its various forms has become the predominant expression of Protestantism.

Lalive d'Epinay, in his now classic study in Chile, shows that Pentecostalism is at once in radical continuity and disjunction with its historical and social contexts. It understands the essence of popular religious practice and gives it new expression while discarding its traditional forms. It rejects the cult of the saints, but affirms the healing power of the spirit; it rejects festival and sacred processions, yet it is very public in its display of religious enthusiasm; it rejects the camaraderie of the cantina and substitutes the fellowship of nightly worship with stirring music, shared testimony, and prayer. Though against institutional systems of authority, clerical, papal, denominational, it asserts the ancient, and no less powerful authority of the cacique. While anyone, by the gift of the Spirit, may emerge as a leader, the selection is not democratic but charismatic. In short, Pentecostal Protestantism represents a fundamental accommodation of the teaching and practice of received traditions and counterposes imposed institutional authority with an authority that grows out of the community itself.[15]

Pentecostalism expresses the real-life experience and struggle of its adherents in forms that are commensurate with their daily experience. Those forms give free expression of the struggle for existence and self-affirmation in environments that are alien to mainline institutions. The community's life is governed by its struggle to solve the problem of survival in an alien environment and is not concerned with the application of programs created elsewhere and mediated through external structures of authority.[16]

Mainline Protestantism may be easily perceived in many sectors of the Hispanic American community as systems of teaching and institutional interests that do not correspond to the life experience of the community. Persons who experience the larger social context as threatening and oppressive may choose a faith expression that recognizes and affirms that experience. If Pentecostal societies do not struggle for systemic transformation through political involvement, they do create an alternative environment that brings a degree of peace and satisfaction to their adherents and sustains them in their struggle with a hostile world. That form of religion may be perceived as an opiate, or it may be acknowledged as a powerful mode of protest to systemic oppression.

A DISTINCTIVE ROLE FOR HISPANIC AMERICAN PROTESTANTISM

Despite the perpetuation of structures and patterns of dependence for Hispanic Protestants and despite their relatively insignificant numbers, they are integral members of the larger community of *La Raza*. Their Protestant affiliation need not be viewed primarily as a means of acculturation or of escape. Hispanic American Protestants now begin to convert the institutions of their oppressors into instruments of service with the oppressed. Institutionally, such a transformation may never be complete, but Hispanic American Protestants are uniquely situated to put the power and resources of the conqueror's institutions to the service of the conquered. That service will be defined increasingly by Hispanic Americans who choose their identity as Hispanics and Christians, even as Protestant Christians.[17]

Hispanic Pentecostalism, problematic in many ways, is itself a fundamental challenge to its environing social contexts, civil and ecclesiastic. Something basic to the assertion of human worth and dignity is expressed in the movement. It cannot simply be dismissed as irrelevant and escapist in relation to the struggle for justice. In it the voice of a people finds expression. It is a voice that must not be ignored.

Increasingly there are signs that an Hispanic church of the people is stirring within the institutions of Protestantism and Roman Catholicism. Though relations between these two great Christian traditions are no less problematic now than in the past, in the complex variety of form and practice there is in continual formation an Hispanic Christian community that is catholic in its concern and ministry, and committed to the embodiment in the flesh of *La Raza* of the suffering love of One who died Servant of all, yet Lord of all, the Sign of the coming liberation of all humankind.

—9—

The Future of the Hispanic Church

The objective — and challenge — of the bishops of the United States has been to build one church out of many ethnic groups. In the main that has happened, though some groups took longer than others to become part of the melting-pot church. Hispanics, however, remain a people apart. They continue to cling to their culture and maintain at least some of their religious traditions. There is "social distance" between them and the institutional Church. For some it is a vague discomfort of not feeling at home. For others, it is the perception that the clergy are not interested in them. Moreover, Hispanics in the main have no role in ministry: episcopal, clerical, religious, or lay. They are the objects of ministry rather than its agents.

Hispanics are largely outside the Church for the same reasons they are still peripheral in society: racism and discrimination still exist. Archbishop Pio Laghi, the apostolic delegate to the United States, reminded the nation's bishops at their annual meeting in 1988 that Hispanics are still discriminated against in the Church. The bias is more subtle than in the past, when people were told bluntly that they were not welcome, but the lack of respect can still be detected.

Hispanics who most need the Church's commitment are often of a lower economic class. This group includes the nearly one-third who live below the poverty line and the refugees and immigrants fleeing war, political persecution, or hunger in Latin

131

America. In 1988, six out of ten Hispanic families were among the two-fifths of the poorest families in the nation.[1] Hispanics also constitute three-fourths of the farmworkers in the nation, one of the most deprived labor forces. Father Joseph Fitzpatrick, a Jesuit sociologist, wrote that middle-class clergy and religious face difficulties in ministering to the poor. That is because class differences touch economic and political concerns, he wrote.[2]

The Catholic Church in the United States, increasingly middle-class in its membership and in its values, has provided the kind of ministry that its class needs. But it has had little to offer a people who are not only of a lower economic class but also a minority for which there has been only a limited place in society. Hispanics with long tenure in the United States have yet to achieve equality. They lack adequate representation in politics, government, industry, business, and education. What Hispanics have needed from the Church is a strong commitment to social justice. That kind of Hispanic ministry has been the option of individuals — bishops, clergy, religious men and women, and laity. But for the most part, ministry to the Hispanics is not the result of structural priorities. Often, bishops, superiors, or provincials provide little backing for those who have chosen to work with Hispanics. Because the work is difficult, some are unable to sustain their efforts, suffering burnout or disillusionment. The corporate response on the part of bishops as well as religious orders and congregations has been long on rhetoric but short on action. That is why little has been done to implement the national pastoral plan for Hispanic ministry approved by the bishops in 1987.

A storefront model of ministry has prevailed; the Church has largely waited for the Hispanics to come for service. From time to time, successful models of an outgoing ministry have appeared, e.g., the Mission Band of California in the 1950s, but they have not been perpetuated and expanded. The attitude has been that special models of ministry for Hispanics are not needed.

This issue, however, is not one-sided; Hispanics bear some responsibility for their alienation. Though a deeply religious people, they lack a strong tradition of priesthood. Many tend to be anticlerical. That is particularly true among Mexicans because the Church in times past often sided with the rich and powerful and failed to speak for the poor. It is also due to machismo, which sees the practice of religion as somehow unmanly, to be left to the women and children. The result is that vocations have not been encouraged in the home.

Socially Hispanics, both citizens and immigrants, are an uprooted people. This includes not just the nearly two million Puerto Ricans who have come to the mainland in the past fifty years and the millions of documented and undocumented immigrants and refugees who have arrived from Latin America in the past three decades. In this category belong also the majority of U. S. Hispanics who early in this century were a rural people and now are the most urbanized ethnic group in the nation. This exodus, originating both externally and internally, has ruptured traditional societies, scattered and divided families not only across state lines but also across international borders. There is a great need to reunite families, reconstruct the community, and find a home.

Because these relocated people saw themselves as sojourners wherever they settled, they did not involve themselves fully in the institutions of society. They thought that they would soon be returning home. Though few can return, many still yearn for their homeland and remain aloof when they should be immersing themselves and creating a new society where they are going to spend their lives.

The most important reason why Hispanics remain a people apart is that they are different from others in the U.S. Church. Though other ethnic groups did encounter short-term discrimination, Hispanics were rejected outright. They underwent a process that left them "colonized," "conquered," "strangers in their own land." The defeatism which is the chief effect of that sad history leaves many unable to associate on an equal basis with members of the majority culture. Though much healing has taken place in recent years, it will be a long time before the process is complete.

For all these reasons, Hispanics remain a group apart in the Church, a condition almost certain to increase in the future despite the Church's hope to serve them better. By the year

2000, according to projections, there will be sixty percent fewer priests than in 1989. Already, a certain triage is becoming evident; wherever parishes are closed, as in Detroit and Chicago, they tend to be the ones serving the minorities. Hispanics in the inner cities are therefore likely to be left without priests.

Yet, little is being done to prepare for that day. While pastors and bishops are interested in developing leadership among Hispanics, what they do is train readers, ministers of the Eucharist, song leaders, and the like. But Hispanics need leadership training of a different kind, as leaders and evangelizers in small ecclesial communities. They need training such as that provided by Communities Organized for Public Service (COPS), which organizes the poor to win political power in the urban barrios. In short, they need training to liberate themselves from the fate of colonized people.

From colonial times, building a Church has been the unfinished task of Hispanics. That process, just beginning in the Southwest when that territory became part of the United States, was resumed a century later when a few structures were established by the Bishops' Committee for the Spanish-speaking: the special office, the councils and, later, the diocesan, regional and national apostolates. Then there were the Spanish-language branches of various movements—the *Cursillo*, Marriage Encounter and the Charismatic movement. Perhaps the most significant has been the Encuentro movement, which led to the preparation of the national pastoral plan for Hispanic ministry. There is no comparable movement for the church as a whole, no national pastoral plan resulting from consultation at the grassroots level.

During the heady days of the *Movimiento*, the Hispanic civil rights movement of the sixties and early seventies, activist priests sometimes talked about a separate Hispanic Church, but this has never really been an option. There have never been the bishops, clergy, and religious to lead such an institution. The only recourse has been to be a leaven and, in that way, create for Hispanics a home within the larger Church. In a sense, with such movements as the *Cursillo* and Marriage Encounter, progress is being made in that direction.

Also, Central and South American refugees may have a significant contribution to make. Among them there are persons who have suffered brutal torture. Some have lost mothers, fathers, brothers, or sisters to the death squads. Some have seen their entire community massacred by the armed forces. Hundreds of thousands have had to flee for their lives. These experiences have irrevocably changed the victims and their religious values.

Suffering, however, is shared by many more than those people described above. This category also includes the so-called economic immigrants, driven by increasing hunger, who enter the country illegally. It includes the hundreds of thousands of farmworkers, citizens of the United States, who have been unable to command a just wage and a work environment safe from dangerous pesticides. It includes the residents of urban slums victimized by the drug lords because they cannot get adequate law enforcement. Certainly the religious value of that suffering can have a purifying effect on the entire Church.

Among the individuals to which the Hispanic Church owes its progress in recent decades are not only a few bishops, clergy, and religious men and women, but also lay persons who have made a true option for the poor and have been able to maintain their commitment in spite of many setbacks. In that long list of lay persons, not all of whom work under auspices of the Church, one has to include Cesar Chavez, the leader of the United Farm Workers; the late Willie Velasquez, who, as head of the Southwest Voter Registration Education Project, dedicated his life to giving Hispanics a political voice; and Ernie Cortez, the organizer of Communities Organized for Public Service in San Antonio and United Neighborhoods Organization in Los Angeles. They are models of commitment not only for the official shepherds of the Church but for the laity as well.

According to demographers, Hispanics will be the majority of the nation's Catholics by the first decade of the coming century. It remains to be seen how they will respond when they are no longer a minority. That change, however, will be only among the laity. Hispanic bishops, clergy, and religious will still be a tiny minority; vocations, while increasing, are not going up sufficiently to make a difference. Nevertheless, the role of the laity, in view of the diminishing numbers of priests, will be paramount. Much more of the Church's ministry will be in their hands. To fulfill that challenge, they will need to develop a strong sense of ownership of the Church, which comes with shared responsibility. That is coming but, alas, too slowly.

Nevertheless, an Hispanic Church, defined not so much by structures as by its character, is beginning to take form. It is one that is "unabashedly affective or emotive,"[3] as the popularity of the charismatic renewal among Hispanics demonstrates. It is one that is in process of developing its own theology, following the pioneering efforts of Father Virgil Elizondo. It is one that has already developed much of its own liturgy, thanks to the work of the Institute of Hispanic Liturgy. It is one where lay leadership has come forward in recent years through the Encuentro Movement, the Hispanic deacon program, and various other movements. Whether the larger Church will accept its contribution is not certain. But one thing is certain: it will endure.

Notes

CHAPTER 2

1. María de Jesus Ybarra, "Los Hispanos en el Noroeste: Primera Migración, 1774–1820," an unpublished paper citing research by Erasmo Gamboa and T.J. St. Hilaire, S.J.

2. Edward P. Dozier, *The Pueblo Indians of North America* (New York: Holt, Rinehart & Winston, 1970), p. 45.

3. Frederick Webb Hodge, George P. Hammond, and Agapito Rey, eds., *Fray Alonso de Benavides' Revised Memorial of 1634* (Albuquerque: The University of New Mexico Press, 1945), p. 68.

4. Ibid., p. 42.

5. Ibid., p. 80.

6. Jay P. Dolan, *The American Catholic Experience: A History from Colonial Times to the Present* (New York: Doubleday, 1985), p. 30.

7. *Encyclopedia Americana*, Vol. II, p. 424.

8. Dolan, *The American Catholic Experience*, p. 26.

9. Ibid., pp. 55–56.

10. David J. Weber, *The Mexican Frontier, 1821–1846: The American Southwest under Mexico* (Albuquerque: University of New Mexico Press, 1982), p. 57.

11. William H. Harris and Judith H. Levy, *The New Columbia Encyclopedia* (New York: Columbia University Press, 1975), p. 1413.

12. Fray Angelico Chavez, *The Old Faith and Old Glory: The Story of the Church in New Mexico since the American Occupation (1846–1946)* (Santa Fe: Santa Fe Press, 1946), p. 3.

13. Dozier, *The Pueblo Indians of North America*, p. 76.

14. Though the Indians were supposed to be the chief beneficiaries of the division of mission properties, the Spaniards or mestizos ended up as the owners.

15. Weber, *The Mexican Frontier*, p. 67.

16. Ibid., p. 44.

17. Dozier, op. cit., pp. 53–54.

18. Weber, op. cit., p. 71.

19. Ibid., p. 71.

20. Jerome J. Martinez y Alire, "The Influence of the Roman Catholic Church in New Mexico under Mexican Administration: 1821–1848," unpublished paper presented at the CEHILA symposium in Las Cruces, New Mexico, in January 1988.

21. Ibid.

22. Weber, op. cit., p. 74.

23. Juan Romero and Moises Sandoval, *Reluctant Dawn: Historia del Padre A.J. Martinez, Cura de Taos* (San Antonio: Mexican American Cultural Center, 1976), p. 11.

24. Ibid., p. 14.

25. Bob Wright, "A Bibliographic Essay on the Catholic Church in the Hispanic Southwest, 1790-1850: Decline of the Missions or Emergence of the Local Church," a paper presented at the CEHILA Symposium at Notre Dame University in March 1989, to be published in revised form in *U.S. Catholic Historian*, Spring 1990.

26. Angelico Chavez, *My Penitente Land: Reflections on Spanish New Mexico* (Albuquerque: University of New Mexico Press, 1966), p. 111.

27. Jerome Martinez y Alire, "The Influence of the Roman Catholic Church," p. 19.

28. Marta Weigle, *The Penitentes of the Southwest* (Santa Fe: Ancient City Press, 1970), p. 18.

CHAPTER 3

1. Jerome Martinez y Alire, "The Influence of the Roman Catholic Church in New Mexico under Mexican Administration," unpublished paper presented at the CEHILA symposium in Las Cruces, New Mexico, in January 1988, p. 16.

2. Kevin Starr, *Americans and the California Dream: 1850–1915* (London: Oxford University Press, 1973), as quoted by Robert Coles in his review, "California, Here I Come," *The New Yorker*, August 6, 1973.

3. Rodolfo Acuña, *Occupied America: A History of Chicanos*, 2nd ed. (New York: Harper and Row, 1981), p. 17.

4. Edwin Sylvest, Jr., "Hispanic American Protestantism in the United States," in Moises Sandoval, ed., *Fronteras: A History of the Latin American Church in the USA since 1513* (San Antonio: the Mexican American Cultural Center, 1983), p. 285.

5. Robert F. Heizer and Alan F. Almquist, *The Other Californians* (Berkeley: University of California Press, 1971), p. 200.

6. Wayne Moquin with Charles van Doren, eds., *A Documentary*

History of the Mexican Americans (New York: Praeger Publishers, 1971), p. 181.

7. Carey McWilliams, *North from Mexico: The Spanish-speaking People of the United States* (New York: Greenwood Press, 1968), p. 110.

8. James A. Michener, *Centennial* (New York: Random House, 1974), p. 926.

9. McWilliams, op. cit., p. 90.

10. Leonardo Pitt, *Decline of the Californios* (Berkeley: University of California Press), p. 117.

11. David F. Gomez, *Somos Chicanos: Strangers in Our Own Land* (Boston: Beacon Press, 1973), p. 50.

12. Ellwyn R. Stoddard, *Mexican Americans* (Washington, D.C.: University Press of America, 1973), p. 5.

13. David J. Weber, *Foreigners in Their Native Land: Historical Roots of the Mexican Americans* (Albuquerque: University of New Mexico Press, 1973), p. 181.

14. Moises Sandoval and Salvador E. Alvarez, "The Church in California," in Sandoval, ed., *Fronteras*, p. 220.

15. Weber, op. cit., p. 145.

16. Fray Angelico Chavez, *The Old Faith and Old Glory* (Santa Fe: Santa Fe Press, 1946), p. 8.

17. Lucien Hendren, "The Church in New Mexico," in Sandoval, ed., *Fronteras*, p. 201, citing the archives of the Archdiocese of Santa Fe.

18. Carmen Tafolla, in Sandoval, ed., *Fronteras*, p. 188.

19. Ibid., p. 189.

20. Ibid., p. 188.

21. Jean A. Meyer, *The Cristero Rebellion, the Mexican People between Church and State 1926–1929* (New York: Cambridge University Press, 1976), p. 6.

22. Carmen Tafolla, op. cit., p. 188.

23. Francis J. Weber, *Catholic Footprints in California* (Newhall, Calif.: Hogarth Press, 1970), pp. 219–220.

24. Ibid., p. 216.

25. Ibid., p. 212.

26. The historian was Michael Neri, cited by Salvador Alvarez and Moises Sandoval, in *Fronteras*, p. 215.

27. Marta Weigle, *The Penitentes of the Southwest* (Santa Fe: Ancient City Press, 1970), p. 14.

28. Frances Leon Swadesh, *Los Primeros Pobladores* (Notre Dame, Ind.: University of Notre Dame Press, 1974), p. 73.

29. Ibid.

30. Ibid., p. 77.

31. Juan Romero and Moises Sandoval, *Reluctant Dawn: Historia del Padre A.J. Martínez, Cura de Taos* (San Antonio: Mexican American Cultural Center, 1976), p. 15, citing Santiago Valdez, "Biografia del Presbitero Antonio José Martínez" (unpublished manuscript in Huntington Library, 1877, Vol. I), p. 96.

32. Ibid., p. 1.

33. Lucien Hendren, "The Church in New Mexico," in *Fronteras*, p. 203.

34. The United States Commission for Civil Rights, *Puerto Ricans in the United States: An Uncertain Future* (Washington, D.C.: October 1976), p. 11.

CHAPTER 4

1. Jay P. Dolan, *The American Catholic Parish: A History from 1850 to the Present* (New York: Paulist Press, 1987), Vol. II, p. 81.

2. Carmen Tafoya, "Expansion of the Church in Texas," in Moises Sandoval, ed., *Fronteras: A History of the Latin American Church in the USA since 1513* (San Antonio: Mexican American Cultural Center, 1983), p. 227.

3. Ibid., p. 235.

4. Ibid., p. 236.

5. Dolan, *The American Catholic Parish*, Vol. II, p. 88.

6. Manuel Gamio, *Mexican American Immigration to the United States: A Study of Human Migration and Adjustment* (New York: Dover Publications, 1971), p. 118.

7. Salvador Alvarez, "The Roots of Mestizo Catholicism in California," in *Fronteras*, p. 243.

8. Dolan, op. cit., p. 83.

9. Alvarez, op. cit., p. 242.

10. Thomas E. Sheridan, *Los Tucsoneros, The Mexican Community in Tucson: 1854–1942* (Tucson: University of Arizona Press, 1986), p. 155.

11. Fray Angelico Chavez, *The Old Faith and Old Glory: The Story of the Church in New Mexico since the American Occupation (1846–1946)* (Santa Fe, New Mexico: The Santa Fe Press, 1946), p. 22.

12. Ibid.

13. Fray Angelico Chavez, as quoted by Juan Romero and Moises Sandoval, *Reluctant Dawn: Historia del Padre A.J. Martinez, Cura de Taos* (San Antonio: Mexican American Cultural Center, 1976), p. 14.

14. Chavez, *The Old Faith*, p. 30.

15. Dolan, *The American Catholic Parish*, p. 85.

16. *Progress Report*, Bishops' Committee for the Spanish-speaking (May 1 to November 1, 1946).

17. Raymond McGowan, "History and Necessity of the Catholic Council for the Spanish-speaking," in Catholic Councils for the Spanish-speaking, *Proceedings of the Tenth Annual Conference* (April 1960), p. 30.

18. U.S. Department of Labor, Bureau of Employment Security.

19. *History of the Immigration and Naturalization Service*, a report prepared by the Senate Judiciary Committee for the Select Commission on Immigration and Refugee Policy, Congressional Research Service (December 1980), p. 2.

20. Leo Grebler, Joan W. Moore, Ralph C. Guzman, *The Mexican American People, the Nation's Second-largest Minority* (New York: The Free Press, 1970), p. 526.

21. Carey McWilliams, *North from Mexico: The Spanish-Speaking People of the United States* (New York: Greenwood Press, 1968), p. 102.

22. Julian Samora, Joe Bernal, and Albert Pena, *Gunpowder Justice: A Reassessment of the Texas Rangers* (South Bend, Ind.: University of Notre Dame Press, 1979), p. 5.

23. Ibid., p. 12, citing T. R. Fehrenbach.

24. Ibid., p. 63.

25. Ibid., p. 1.

26. Paul S. Taylor, *Mexican Labor in the United States* (Berkeley, Calif.: University of California Press, 1932), Vol. 8, p. 27.

27. Ibid., p. 134.

28. Gamio, *Mexican Immigration*, p. 119.

29. Antonio M. Stevens Arroyo, "Puerto Rican Migration to the United States," in *Fronteras*, p. 274.

30. Carey McWilliams, *Ill Fares the Land: Migrants and Migratory Labor in the United States* (Boston: Little, Brown and Co., 1942), p. 158.

31. Armando Morales, *Ando Sangrando: A Study of Mexican American-Police Conflict* (La Puente, Calif.: Perspective Publications, 1974), p. 34; National Commission on Law Observance and Enforcement, *Report on Crime and the Foreign Born* (United States Government, 1931), p. 230.

32. McWilliams, *North from Mexico*, p. 248.

33. Mary Gordon, "I Can't Stand Your Books: A Writer Goes Home," *New York Times Review of Books* (December 11, 1988), pp. 1ff.

34. Rodolfo Acuña, *Occupied America: The Chicano's Struggle Toward Liberation* (San Francisco: Canfield Press, 1972), p. 166.

35. Alberto Camarillo, "Mexican American and Non-Profit Organ-

izations," a paper presented at the conference on Hispanics and the Independent Sector, University of San Francisco (November 14–16, 1988), p. 4.

36. Cf. Carey McWilliams, *North from Mexico*, pp. 189ff.

CHAPTER 5

1. Juan Romero, "History of PADRES," paper delivered at the symposium sponsored by the Commission of Historical Studies of the Church in Latin America (CEHILA) at Las Cruces, N.M., January 15–17, 1988.

2. David Gomez, *Somos Chicanos: Strangers in Our Own Land* (Boston: Beacon Press, 1973), p. 9.

3. Paul Baca, "Preparation of Hispanic Priests for the United States," a talk given at the First National Encuentro, June 12, 1972, Washington, D.C. Though Baca did not mention the name of the archbishop in his talk, he later told the author it was Vehr.

4. Moises Sandoval, *Our Legacy: The First 50 Years*, a history of the first fifty years of the League of United Latin American Citizens (Washington, D.C.: League of United Latin American Citizens, 1979), p. 38.

5. James Dolan in a talk at the Newark hearing of U.S. Bishops' Call to Action, on "Ethnicity and Race," December 4–6, 1975.

6. Leo Grebler, Joan W. Moore, Ralph C. Guzman, *The Mexican American People: the Nation's Second-largest Minority* (New York: The Free Press, 1970), p. 456.

7. Tony Castro, *Chicano Power: The Emergence of Mexican America* (New York: E.P. Dutton, 1974), p.107.

8. Moises Sandoval, in *Fronteras: A History of the Latin American Church in the USA since 1513* (San Antonio: Mexican American Cultural Center, 1983), p. 371.

9. Ibid.

10. Ibid.

11. Ibid., p. 398.

12. Ibid., p. 399.

13. Ibid., p. 406.

14. Ibid.

15. Ibid., pp. 406–407.

16. Francis J. Furey, interviewed by author.

17. Ibid.

18. James Hennessey, *American Catholics: A History of the Roman Catholic Community of the United States* (New York: Oxford University Press, 1981), p. 325.

19. Antonio M. Stevens Arroyo, *Prophets Denied Honor: An Anthology of the Hispanic Church in the United States* (Maryknoll, NY: Orbis, 1980), pp. 176–177 passim.

20. Report of the Citizens Advisory Panel to the Governor of New Mexico, September 1980, p. 2.

21. The quote about being "beat at our own game" is attributed to Father Vicente Lopez, a prominent member of PADRES, in Juan Romero, "History of PADRES," op. cit., p. 34.

22. Sandoval, in *Fronteras*, p. 429, citing proceedings of the First National Encuentro.

23. Ibid., p. 430, citing James V. Casey, "Church Concerned," *Denver Catholic Register*, March 29, 1973, p. 3.

24. This is what officials of the USCC estimated the Third Encuentro process cost, including the diocesan, regional, and national encuentros, plus the various meetings of the committees involved.

25. Martin McMurtrey, *Mariachi Bishop: The Life Story of Patrick Flores* (San Antonio: Corona Publishing Co., 1987), p. 51.

26. Sandoval, in *Fronteras*, p. 453.

27. Moises Sandoval, "Hispanic Challenges to the Church," a paper prepared for the Secretariat for Hispanic Affairs, United States Catholic Conference, June 1978, p. 54.

CHAPTER 6

1. Population Reference Bureau, "The Hispanic Population: Current Demographic Trends," a document prepared by Wendy Patriquin for a briefing of the U.S. Catholic Conference, February 5, 1988.

2. "Hispanic Population of the United States," *Clergy Report*, Vol. 18, No. 4, April 1988, p. 7.

3. Robert O. Gonzalez and Michael La Velle, *The Hispanic Catholic in the United States: A Socio-Cultural and Religious Profile* (New York: Northeast Pastoral Center for Hispanics, 1985), p. 180; "A Gallup Study of Religious and Social Attitudes of Hispanic Americans," conducted for *Our Sunday Visitor*, The Gallup Organization, Inc., August 1978. The Gonzales-La Valle study showed that 54 percent of Hispanics attended Mass regularly, a response thought to have been influenced by the way the question was asked.

4. Moises Sandoval, ed., *Fronteras: A History of the Latin American Church in the USA since 1513* (San Antonio: Mexican American Cultural Center, 1983), p. 415.

5. Ibid., p. 420.

6. James Dolan, *The American Catholic Experience: A History from*

Colonial Times to the Present (New York: Doubleday, 1985), p. 375.

7. Sandoval, *Fronteras*, p. 368.

8. Ibid., p. 418.

9. Ibid., p. 450.

10. Moises Sandoval, "Hispanic Challenges to the Church," a paper published by the Secretariat for Hispanic Affairs, United States Catholic Conference, June 1978, p. 54.

11. Ibid., p. 38.

12. Bishop Patricio Flores, "The Church: Diocesan and National," a talk delivered at the First National Encuentro, Washington, D.C., June 19-22, 1972.

13. Sandoval, *Fronteras*, p. 383.

14. Ibid.

15. Ibid., p. 380.

16. Ibid., p. 383.

17. Ibid.

18. Ibid., p. 386.

19. Ibid., p. 387.

20. Interview by author in 1986.

CHAPTER 7

1. Juan Clark, *Why? The Cuban Exodus: Background, Evolution and Impact in U.S.A.* (Miami: Union of Cubans in Exile, 1977), p. 16.

2. Bryan O. Walsh, "The Spanish Impact Here: How the Archdiocese Is Meeting the Challenge," *The Voice*, July 18, 1975.

3. Bryan O. Walsh, "The Church and the City: The Miami Experience," in *New Catholic World*, published in early 1980s, exact date unknown.

4. Juan Clark, "Cuban Exodus Fact Sheet," undated.

5. Bryan O. Walsh, op. cit., July 18, 1975.

6. *Puerto Ricans in the Continental United States: An Uncertain Future*, a report of the U.S. Commission on Civil Rights, October 1976, p. 18.

7. Ibid.

8. *The Hispanic Community, the Church and the Northeast Center for Hispanics* (New York: Northeast Catholic Pastoral Center for Hispanics, 1982), p. 19.

9. Fran Gillespie, "Hispanics in the U.S. Labor Force: A Briefing Presented to the U.S. Catholic Conference," February 5, 1988, citing "The Hispanic Population in the United States: March 1986 and 1987 (Advance Report)" by U.S. Department of Commerce, Bureau of the

Census, *Current Population Reports*, August 1987.

10. Paul Sedillo, "Liberty and Justice for All," San Antonio hearing of Call to Action, p. 17 of proceedings.

11. *The Hispanic Community*, op. cit., p. 5.

12. Wayne Cornelius, *Mexican Migration to the United States: Causes, Consequences and U.S. Responses*, Migration and Development Study Group, Center for Migration Studies, Massachusetts Institute of Technology, Cambridge, Mass., 1978, pp. 4–5.

13. Wayne A. Cornelius, "Illegal Mexican Migration to the United States: Recent Research Findings, Policy Implications and Research Priorities," Center for International Studies, Massachusetts Institute of Technology, Cambridge, Mass., May 1977, pp. 2–3.

14. Ibid., p. 4.

15. Allan Figueroa Deck, S.J., "A Christian Perspective on the Reality of Illegal Immigration," a talk given to the Priests' Senate of the Diocese of San Diego, February 15, 1978, p. 11.

16. Because Puerto Ricans have been citizens since 1917, they are not technically immigrants, but their experience on the mainland has been the same as if they had been foreigners.

CHAPTER 8

1. R. Douglas Brackenridge and Francisco O. Garcia-Treto, *Iglesia Presbiteriana: A History of Presbyterians and Mexican Americans in the Southwest* (San Antonio: Trinity University Press, 1974), p. 3.

2. Ibid., pp. 6–7.

3. Melinda Rankin, *Twenty Years Among the Mexicans: A Narrative of Missionary Labor* (Cincinnati: Chase and Hall, Publishers, 1875).

4. Thomas Herwood, *History of New Mexico Spanish and English Missions of the Methodist Episcopal Church from 1850 to 1910*, 2 vols. (Albuquerque: El Abogado Press, 1908–1910), I, p. 22.

5. Alfredo Nañez, *Historia de la Conferencia Rio Grande de la Iglesia Metodista Unida* (Dallas: Bridwell Library, Southern Methodist University, 1981), pp. 44–47.

6. Brackenridge and Garcia-Treto, *Iglesia Presbiteriana*, p. 26.

7. Justo L. Gonzalez, *The Development of Christianity in the Latin Caribbean* (Grand Rapids: Eerdmans, 1969), pp. 91–95.

8. Elmer T. Clark, *The Latin Immigrant in the South* (Nashville: The Cokesbury Press, 1924). Clark, a denominational executive of the Methodist Episcopal Church, South, expressed an attitude held by many Anglos who intended well. "Socially the Cuban immigrant is of a better class than the Mexican. . . . It is not to be thought, however, that these

Cuban immigrants are of such a high type that they can immediately take their places in American social life. Such is far from the case. They come from the Catholic environment ... and for the most part they are poor, ignorant and superstitious; it is not to be expected that immigrants from a land wherein more than half the people are illiterate would be of the highest type. These Cubans, almost as much as the Mexicans, need the social and religious ministry of the Protestant Church," pp. 51–52.

9. Quoted in Brackenridge and Garcia-Treto, *Iglesia Presbiteriana*, p. 128. Cf. Vernon M. McCombs, *From Over the Border* (New York: Council of Women for Home Missions and Missionary Education Movement, 1925), p. 83.

10. Ibid., p. 117.

11. Jose Moreno Fernandez, *Hispanic Methodism in the Southern California Arizona Conference* (The School of Theology at Claremont, unpublished Rel.D. dissertation, 1973), pp. 85–86; Alfredo Nañez, *Historia*, pp. 87–89.

12. Brackenridge and Garcia-Treto, *Iglesia Presbiteriana*, p. 84.

13. Leo D. Nieto, "The Chicano Movement and the Churches in the United States," *Perkins Journal*, 29 (Fall 1975), p. 27.

14. Nieto, "The Chicano Movement and the Churches," p. 37.

15. Christian Lalive d'Epinay, *El Refugio de las Masas: Estudio Sociologico del Protestantismo Chileno* (Santiago: Editorial del Pacifico, S. A., 1968). Cf. Jean Pierre Bastian, *Breve Historia del Protestantismo en America Latina* (Mexico, D.F.: Casa Unida de Publicaciones, S.A., 1986), pp. 164–167.

16. Lalive d'Epinay, *El Refugio*, p. 96.

17. David Maldonado, "Chicano Protestantism: A Conceptual Perspective" (Arlington, TX: mimeographed paper, 1975), pp. 12–13.

CHAPTER 9

1. "Shortchanged: Recent Developments in Hispanic Poverty, Income and Employment," a report by the Center for Budget and Policy Studies, Washington, D. C., 1988.

2. Joseph P. Fitzpatrick, "The Hispanic Poor in a Middle-Class Church," *America,* July 2, 1988, p. 12.

3. Allan Figueroa Deck, "Proselytism and Hispanic Catholics: How Long Do We Cry Wolf?" *America* (Dec. 10, 1988), pp. 485ff.

Bibliography

Acuña, Rodolfo. *Occupied America: A History of Chicanos* (2nd ed.). New York: Harper and Row, 1981.

Chavez, Fray Angelico. *My Penitente Land: Reflections on Spanish New Mexico*. Albuquerque: University of New Mexico Press, 1974.

————. *The Old Faith and Old Glory: The Story of the Church in New Mexico since the American Occupation (1843–1946)*. Santa Fe, N.M.: Sante Fe Press, 1946.

Clark, Juan. *Why? The Cuban Exodus: Background, Evolution and Impact in U.S.A.* Miami: Union of Cubans in Exile, 1977.

Deck, Allan Figueroa. *The Second Wave: Hispanic Ministry and the Evangelization of Cultures*. New York: Paulist Press, 1989.

Dolan, Jay P. (ed.). *The American Catholic Parish: A History from 1850 to the Present*. New York: Paulist Press, 1987.

————. *The American Catholic Experience: A History from Colonial Times to the Present*. Garden City, N.Y.: Doubleday, 1985.

Dunne, John Gregory. *Delano: The Story of the California Grape Strike*. New York: Farrar, Straus & Giroux, 1967.

Dussel, Enrique. *Historia General de la Iglesia en America Latina*. Vol. I, *Introducción General*. Salamanca, Spain: Ediciones Sigueme, 1983.

Gamio, Manuel. *Mexican American Immigration to the United States: A Study of Human Migration and Adjustment*. New York: Dover Publications, 1971.

Gomez, David F. *Somos Chicanos: Strangers in Our Own Land*. Boston: Beacon Press, 1973.

Grebler, Leo, Joan W. Moore, Ralph C. Guzman. *The Mexican American People: The Nation's Second-largest Minority*. New York: The Free Press, 1970.

Hennesey, James. *American Catholics: A History of the Roman Catholic Community in the United States*. New York: Oxford University Press, 1981.

The Hispanic Community, the Church and the Northeast Center for Hispanics, a report by the Northeast Pastoral Center for Hispanics, New York, N.Y., 1982.

147

Holland, Clifton L. *The Religious Dimension in Hispanic Los Angeles: A Protestant Case Study*. South Pasadena, Calif.: William Carey Library, 1974.

Hurtado, Juan. *Social Distance Between the Mexican American and the Church*. San Antonio: Mexican American Cultural Center, 1975.

McMurtrey, Martin. *Mariachi Bishop: The Life Story of Patrick Flores*. San Antonio: Corona Publishing Co., 1987.

Meier, Matt S., Feliciano Rivera. *The Chicanos: A History of Mexican Americans*. New York: Hill and Wang, 1972.

Meyer, Jean A. *The Cristero Rebellion: The Mexican People Between Church and State 1926–1929*. London: Cambridge University Press, 1976.

Mosqueda, Lawrence J. *Chicanos, Catholicism and Political Ideology*. New York: University Press of America, 1986.

Perez, Arturo. *Popular Catholicism: A Hispanic Perspective*. Washington, D.C.: The Pastoral Press, 1988.

Puerto Ricans in the Continental United States: An Uncertain Future, a report of the U.S. Commission on Civil Rights, October 1976.

Romero, Juan, with Moises Sandoval. *Reluctant Dawn: Historia del Padre A.J. Martinez, Cura de Taos*. San Antonio: Mexican American Cultural Center, 1976.

Sandoval, Moises (ed.). *Fronteras: A History of the Latin American Church in the USA since 1513*. San Antonio, Texas: Mexican American Cultural Center, 1983.

Stevens Arroyo, Antonio M. *Prophets Denied Honor: An Anthology of the Hispanic Church in the United States*. Maryknoll, N.Y.: Orbis, 1980.

Swadesh, Francis Leon. *Los Primeros Pobladores: Hispanic Americans of the Ute Frontier*. South Bend, Ind.: University of Notre Dame Press, 1974.

Weber, David J. (ed.). *Foreigners in Their Native Land: Historical Roots of the Mexican Americans*. Albuquerque: University of New Mexico Press.

Weigle, Marta. *The Penitentes of the Southwest*. Santa Fe, N.M.: Ancient City Press, 1970.

Index